Something
of
Your Own

Something
of
Your Own

Judy Peterson

VICTOR BOOKS®

A DIVISION OF SCRIPTURE PRESS PUBLICATIONS INC.
USA CANADA ENGLAND

Scripture quotations are from the *Holy Bible, New International Version,* © 1973, 1978, 1984, International Bible Society. Used by permission of Zondervan Bible Publishers.

Library of Congress Cataloging-in-Publication Data

Peterson, Judy.
    Something of your own / by Judy Peterson.
      p.   cm.
    ISBN 0-89693-898-0
    1. Women—United States—Psychology. 2. Self-realization.
3. Small business—United States—Planning. 4. Success in business—
United States. I. Title.
    HQ1206.P427 1991
    155.6'33—dc20   91-3237
                                                      CIP

© 1991 by SP Publications, Inc.
Printed in the United States of America

1 2 3 4 5 6 7 8 9 10 Printing/Year 95 94 93 92 91

Contents

for my family

Len

Scott and Misha

Sheri and Keith

Preface

Many years ago, before I was married, I read a moving book, *Gift From the Sea*. In it, Anne Morrow Lindbergh spoke of women looking for new patterns of living because their spirits were going dry. Her answer to this was to find creative work, something that could feed their centers and give them strength.

I believe that women today still have a need to find creative work that will nourish their spirits. My own life would suggest that this is so.

Twice in my life I have felt a strong desire to find purposeful activity. The first time, I was facing an empty nest and wondering what to do with the next part of my life. Nothing had prepared me for that challenge. After carefully thinking about what I could do, I started a business venture and stayed with it for some years, until I sold it and a second time went in search of a creative activity that would satisfy and refill me.

While conducting my search, I became increasingly aware of other women who were looking for the same things as I—fuller use of their talents, activities that could embrace those talents, and, for many, God's direction for their lives. These women were eager, even desperate, to find resolution of these heartfelt concerns. I was moved that women were still struggling with what to do with their lives and resources. I sensed too that I was not alone.

This book represents my journey, and perhaps yours, to

find a creative work. The following pages will show you how to move from personal vision to the development of a Life/Work. This journey may take longer than you expected—a month or two, a year or two. At stake could be a life of growth and meaning.

I hope that *Something of Your Own* will help you on your journey toward the growth of mind, heart, and talent you desire.

Judy Peterson
Boston, Massachusetts
1991

Part One

Chapter One

Discovering Your Personal Path

Gail wonders what she will do with her life now that her children are grown. She works with children who have special needs, but she would like to further develop her interests and talents. Her desire to do this is becoming a driving force in her life.

"I have to go back to addressing what I want to do with my life, especially now that my children are grown. Even my husband is concerned about who he will come home to, what we will have to talk about. He is very involved in work and in several other activities. I really have no excuses now, and I would like to be interesting and growing myself. So I took my desire and, in fear and trembling, I asked God, 'What do You want me to do, and what are the talents I have?' I want to be available when my girls come home to visit and so would like an activity that is flexible. I was really saying to God, 'Where do I fit in within the workplace? What gifts have You given me that can be developed more?' It's my hope to use my abilities to help others and glorify God the best way I can."

Gail is searching for ways to fill her need for purposeful work and for using the talents God has given her. She is thinking of picking up on a dream she has had of writing for children. "I would like to give children hope and express that hope in stories with a spiritual viewpoint."

What about you? Have you ever wondered, like Gail, about the abilities God has given you, how you could use them, or what activity could employ your talents? If so, you share a quest that is more common than you might suspect. The longing to use one's talents and to grow is one that is not apt to go away; if anything, it will only intensify with passing years.

Leslie has also thought about how to use her own resources and has already started the venture she thinks is perfect for her. This, however, was preceded by a period of intense searching.

"I knew in my heart that God had something special for me. In college I secured degrees in art and psychology and liked both. A professor said to me, 'I don't know what you are going to do for your life's work, but it is imperative you surround yourself with people's needs.' I remember thinking that was a funny thing for him to say. Later his comment would still speak to me. With my art background, I thought of interior design, but it did not hold much interest for me. I kept looking for what I could do that would be satisfying. In the meantime I developed a friendship with a seventy-year-old woman named Anne. She was lonely and I would visit her and take her out. Then in June of 1987 she was killed in a car accident. I was devastated and wanted to do something for her family. I took them a rose bush to plant in their yard in memory of Anne. A year later around the anniversary of Anne's death, I heard the rose bush had died, and so I purchased another and dropped it off. As I drove away I thought, 'God, I love doing this kind of thing. There has to be a way to do this as work, or as a job. Please show me!'

"At home that evening, my husband suddenly said, *'Send a Friend.* That could be the name for your idea and your venture, Leslie; you need to be that friend that people will hire to go in their place.'

"Electricity went off in our house. I literally started screaming, because I knew this was it. The concept for my activity began to form. I would visit children in hospitals, adults in nursing homes and retirement centers, shut-ins and those at home recuperating; I would take someone out to lunch or shopping; I would entertain wives who accompanied their husbands on business trips, represent companies at groundbreaking ceremonies, help with open houses.

"Send a Friend was born. I used a rose as my logo to remind me of Anne and how this all got started. My venture would be a natural extension of myself. *Send a Friend* is several months old now, and doing well. I believe it provides an opportunity and a privilege or way to meet the needs and cares of people out there who are lonely, ill, or in some way just need a friend."

Leslie is off to an incredible beginning. In seeing what she had done so professionally in such a short time, I was impressed. Even more exciting was to see her expressing the very essence of herself, making it part of her daily work and life.

A Happening
The wish to creatively express one's abilities in work, activities, or hobbies, is inherent in each of us. Our talents clamor to be used. We see this desire reflected in the numbers of women who have decided to become entrepreneurs, go to work, or have a professional career. The U.S. Small Business Administration tells us that the number of self-employed women has grown from 1.7 million in 1977 to an amazing 4.1 million and rising in the 1990s. One out of every four businesses are now owned by women. Most of these women are in their early forties, have worked for at least seven years in their previous jobs, and have started ventures in various service sectors of the economy. In addition, the estimated total of women-owned enterprises managed from within the home ranges anywhere from 1.2 million to 3 million.

While vast numbers of women have chosen entrepreneurship, others have taken jobs. Women now comprise 45.2 percent of the labor force, with 57.4 percent of the women's population working or looking for employment. A *Mademoiselle*[1] survey asked 10,000 readers, "Who will you be tomorrow?" They found many women wanted to work for at least thirty years. Younger women wanted to find a meaningful job—not just anything would do.

In another study of 300 women ranging in age from thirty-five to fifty-five, in occupations from homemakers to lawyers, researchers Baruch, Barnett and Rivers reported that women now consider doing and achieving as important as relationships and feelings.[2]

A *Time* special issue, "Women: The Road Ahead," stated that many women in the 1990s "want to be independent contractors, working at home at their own hours."[3] Increasingly, women are searching for new ways to use their own resources and to be productive. Women such as Gail and Leslie are no exception, as they look for creative activities and fuller use of their talents, bringing to that effort the added dimension of faith and seeking God's direction for their lives.

More is going on here than businesses being opened or the workforce expanding. Women who want to capitalize on their own talents are causing a happening, an event itself worthy of attention. This is because women, we are told, have not always had the courage to develop their own persons and take charge of their lives. Do you remember *The Feminine Mystique*,[4] published in 1963, or more recently, *The Cinderella Complex*?[5] Both books leveled the same accusation: that women avoided using their minds and abilities and remained at the child/woman stage. In one case it was a "mystique" in society that held them back; in the other, inner networks of fear.

But today, we see vast numbers of women stepping out with courage and imagination. What is occurring lately has less to do with business and labor statistics and more to do with women coming of age. Women are growing into their own fullness as persons, and are using their abilities and minds to do whatever they have in their hearts and minds to do. They are realizing that there are other aspects of being a woman in addition to, but not replacing, being wife and mother. Many women today are actively looking for answers to help them live productively.

A Quest

What woman hasn't asked at some point in her life: "What can I do with my talents that will fill my days and myself, make me feel useful, and be personally rewarding?"

This question is really no different for the Christian woman, for women everywhere are faced with the challenges that life in the 1990s presents. We all live in the same world and are subject to the same vicissitudes, both good and bad.

Judy is a woman who wants to find interesting or rewarding activities. She is happy as a wife, and mother of two grown girls; those roles are both special and important to her. While she plans to continue to give high attention to her home, she is also thinking about what else she could undertake.

"I still hope to find exactly what it is God wants me to do. I have a love for people and want to help others. In terms of thinking of my talents, I took a degree in nursing and social rehabilitation. For a while I was also in a Gift Connection business, helping people shop or shopping for them, but after two years I just didn't care for that. I then bought a bookstore, but found that working a sixty-hour week was too much, especially with a family, so I sold the store.

"I don't want a full-time job, but I have thought of volunteer work. I even went to Massachusetts General Hospital and interviewed for a position. They decided I could do spiritual counseling, because of my background. I tried it for one day! I guess it put me too much in touch with sickness and with my own mortality.

"Right now I am planning to use my background in psychology, my interest in genealogy and the Bible, to write a

genealogy tracing three generations on my father's side of
the family. Then I'll do my mother's. I'd like to understand
my family and myself more. I believe that God has a plan
for me and for my life. Through prayer and understanding
I'll come to know what I should be doing."

Judy has many talents, as her interests evidence. She is
trying new activities, and is open to the leading of God,
looking for what is right for her. Judy is representative, as
are Gail and Leslie, of women who are seeking a worthwhile endeavor or work to be engaged in.

And so is Linda. She has some special challenges as she
thinks about what she wants for her future. She is looking
at those challenges with a good perspective—and they
aren't becoming obstacles to her.

"I've been divorced for five years and have single-
parented the last four of my five children. My current job
as a school nurse and health teacher is a necessity for
survival, but it's not what I want to do. I feel as though my
life is on hold until my children are grown. Also, because
of the abuse the children encountered growing up, I anticipate a longer period of time in which they will need my
support. I want to be there to give it, but I am also very
anxious to get on with the next part of my life. I see it as a
whole new beginning. My dream is to work either in a
foreign field or in this country with the poor. I have a
masters in counseling/psychology and a degree in nursing,
skills I want to share with other people. I believe I can also
offer the continuing internal healing that I experienced as I
became a therapist.

"I do have a conflict with the American expectation of
financial security in older years. This differs from possibly
having to give up a great deal to serve others. I have a
strong desire to be involved in feeding and caring for people who are hurting and without hope. Right now, the
whole transition from parenting to living an independent
lifestyle, however, is a very intense and frightening experience. All of a sudden my focus is off raising children and

on who I am and what I want out of my life.

"I am excited about the prospects of living out my dreams and of creating a new future, and I look forward to God's leading. I don't know what direction I will go, but even the unknown is exciting. The primary challenges are within myself—trusting God, not going ahead of Him, not being afraid to do something God might be leading me to do that I don't have confidence in, or of having more internal healing yet to be accomplished. Nevertheless I really am positive about my future."

A Personal Pathway

Increased awareness of what it means to be women, the multiple choices that are now available and the increased demands of what it takes to survive in today's world are causing women to ask demanding questions:

● "How can I respond creatively to change around me, assume responsibility for my life, and grow as a woman?"

● "How can I discover new ways to use the abilities I have?"

● "Does God really have something special that I can do that will use the many talents He has given me and that will help me adjust to an ever-changing world and my role as a woman?"

I too have asked these questions and faced their challenges both with excitement and trepidation. I started asking them seriously when the younger of my children, my daughter, went away to school sooner than expected. With an empty house and time on my hands, I knew I had to figure out how to spend the half-lifetime still ahead of me.

More and more I came to feel useless and discouraged, for each day presented the task of discovering a purpose or an activity I could enjoy and believe in. Eventually my compelling desire to find a creative outlet that would give my life meaning could not be denied. I didn't want to let webs of fear hold me back and make me a victim.

At the time my husband and I owned a business that

produced glass Christmas ornaments. Starting a custom-crafted gift ornament line of our own, taking advantage of the expertise and facilities we already had to design and market such a line, seemed a natural extension. I decided to start an independent company called Mill Falls Studio that specialized in making high-quality ornaments similar to Hallmark's. Our ornaments were commissioned, designed, and personally created by American artists.

Mill Falls gradually produced a product with nationwide distribution and recognition. One highlight was the Bing Crosby Christmas keepsake ornament, planned in conjunction with Kathryn Crosby. We even had a "Christmas in August" in New York City, complete with horse, carriage and Santa Claus driver, an event covered by the media. After a ride around the block of the St. Regis Hotel, I presented to Kathryn the first of the Bing Crosby ornaments in a special ceremony. It was a unique moment. As my business grew, I was constantly exposed to new experiences that gave me greater confidence and revealed abilities I didn't know I had. Five years later, as my husband and I chose to concentrate on other areas, we sold the ornament company and, along with it, Mill Falls.

Once again I faced the question: What could I be involved in that would be unique and would take advantage of my resources? By now I had a better understanding of myself. There is nothing like self-definition to uncover one's own interests and talents. My search to discover what I could do next became a personal journey, as I slowly began to follow the path on which my own concerns, talents, and God were leading me. I wanted to discover some kind of activity, entrepreneurial in character, personal in design, and God-inspired, that could draw on my creativities. This was not to be an easy path but it was to be a rewarding one. Never before have I done anything so connected to myself, and never before have I so put myself, and God's plans for me, to the test.

Figuring out what I wanted to do with my life, and looking more closely at my own capabilities and my relationship to God, took more time and effort than I had ever counted on. This was a journey I felt I had no choice but to take. It culminated in the writing of this book.

A Challenge

The desire to find a creative outlet for one's talents is one that the years don't diminish; they only add a different and a timely emphasis. As women today are conducting their search, they are increasingly careful about the choices they make in regard to it. There are reasons for their caution. They speak of not having enough time and energy left over for a personal life or for their families, and they don't want to repeat the errors of the past decade with its emphasis on fast-track careers or full-time involvement to the point of exhaustion.

Faith Popcorn, founder of Brain Reserve, a marketing and consulting firm, and known for her ability to predict trends, claims that in the 1990s women will spend more time at home and will concentrate on their families. Women who do work will seek to create entrepreneurial roles at or close to home, allowing them time for the traditional roles of wife and mother.

Women today dream "that they will be the ones to strike a healthy balance at last between their public and private lives. . . ." They are "eager to achieve their goals without sacrificing their natures."[6]

Women today face the challenge of pioneering these new and more flexible roles. We can broaden and define anew what we want to accomplish now and in the years ahead, rethinking issues of work, of what it means to be a woman, and questions of our faith.

Webster tells us a pioneer is one who "originates or helps open up a new line of thought or activity; opens or prepares a way for others to follow."[7]

To pioneer, women will have to think of themselves as capable of "opening up a new line of thought or activity,"

or of "opening or preparing a way for others to follow."

Work can be redefined and enlarged to include opportunities and purposes that go beyond the narrow definition of job, business, or career. With such an approach, the phrase, Life/Work, offers a broader opportunity to create a sane balance between personal and professional goals. Accomplishing this is quite a task, but one that deserves our best efforts and dedication. Fulfillment of our abilities does not have to be marked by a lack of caring for others or by literally going off and "doing our own thing." We can show a sense of responsibility in our life decisions, as we balance the needs of home and vocation.

A Call
You may be searching for ways to put your own abilities and skills to greater use, or to center your activities closer to home. You may not be sure yet what you would like to do; you may want to have a full-time, full-scale career or business, but you may prefer an entrepreneurial role or activity close to or in your home, as an "independent contractor" working at your own hours. This activity or

project could be one done around your tasks as homemaker, at your own discretion and as time permits. The effort could be small scale, and either for profit or social service/volunteer and nonprofit oriented.

You may find yourself desiring to take a slower journey down a broader path that allows you to try many avenues while still having time for family, for other people, or for church life. If you are looking for a meaningful Life/Work and looking also for God's direction for your life, you may be ready to take a creative journey of your own. This journey will require discovering first the abilities God gave you, and second, a vision or dream of ways you could put those abilities to greater use. Your journey will culminate in designing the Life/Work or venture that is ideal for you. It can be anything you want, limited only by your own imagination and desires and by God's plans for you!

You may ask, "Is this possible? Can I actually follow my dreams and goals until they take form and shape and finally do come true?" With a strong commitment and faith on your part, that can happen. This book will serve as a guide on your journey to find a Life/Work you can truly enjoy and find rewarding. As you read you will see a constant interweaving of four different tools and support systems:

1. Self-definition exercises
2. Stories of other women
3. Strategies and principles of business
4. Spiritual or inspirational principles

These exercises, stories, strategies, and principles will assist you, as you travel along. In the very beginning, self-definition and self-knowledge will be necessary before you can discover and design your own creative Life/Work. Most of us have as much need of nuts and bolts assistance for *self-discovery* as we do for *activity discovery*. At other times, women's stories will offer comradeship, understanding, and support. Business strategies will be gradually introduced as you begin to carry out the more practical tasks you face, especially in the latter part of the journey.

Your journey will be one of faith, even the testing of that faith, as you learn to trust God for your own life and future. You will gradually fill out a Life/Work Chart that will help you answer questions about who you are, where you are going, what you want to do with your life, and how you plan to get there. The chart appears in this chapter to give you an idea of the journey you will be taking.

Another Search in Another Time

Over thirty-five years ago Anne Morrow Lindbergh wrote her treasured *Gift from the Sea*. She too was searching, and wondered whether there were other women seeking a new way of living. She felt there was a need for renewal—a need that still exists today. She encouraged women to:

consciously encourage those pursuits which oppose the centrifugal forces of today: quiet time alone, contemplation, prayer, music, a centering line of thought or reading, of study or work. It can be physical or intellectual or artistic, any creative life proceeding from oneself. It need not be an enormous project or a great work. But it should be something of one's own.[8]

It was in 1955 when Anne Lindbergh boldly suggested that, except for children, women's creations were for the most part invisible. Women very much needed to discover other forms of creative expression, or they were in danger of having their spirits go dry, with nothing to refresh or refill them. They needed "something" to provide that refilling on an ongoing basis.

As women living in the 1990s, we have picked up the challenge Anne Morrow Lindbergh gave us so many years ago. More than ever we need to find a visible creation to nourish us. That search continues with a renewed urgency and resolve. Let's journey together to give birth to our visible creations, something of our own that we can draw upon, and that will fulfill and satisfy us.

MY LIFE/WORK CHART

I. Who am I?

A. My purpose/mission/motivation
B. My resources/abilities
C. My uniqueness

II. Where Do I Want To Go?

A. My creative dream of what I'd like to do with my life.
B. My focused dream goal of what I want to become or do.

III. How Can I Get There?

A. My best strategy for getting where I want to go.
B. My risk/reward ratio
   1. What I feel I have to offer or can risk.
   2. What I feel I have to gain.
C. A description of the type of activity I feel could present an acceptable risk factor.

IV. My Creative Activity or Life/Work

A. The definition of my "ideal" activity
B. The purpose of my venture

V. The Charter For My Life/Work Activity

Restate the purpose or goal of my venture. This purpose should be compatible with my declared mission and goals. It is my charter, or road map, for the future.

Chapter Two

Engaging Your Heart with a Vision

For we are God's workmanship, created in Christ
Jesus to do good works, which God prepared in advance for us to do.

Ephesians 2:10

As you prepare to start your journey you may recall a wish
you made as a child, a compliment a teacher gave, or a
statement made in one of your bolder moments, "Someday
I am going to do something special." What have you
dreamed of doing? This is the time to find out what excites
you, what could challenge your abilities more than anything has before.

At some point in our lives we all harbor a secret desire
to commit ourselves passionately to an interest, a cause, or
a dream. During such times that desire may make us rest-
less, at other times hopeful, but more often than not we
are left feeling frustrated or unfulfilled. These strong desires, however, hold the key to our success. Without them,
we never find the courage to begin.

Some time ago I was involved in a seminar in New England for women who wanted to discover an activity they
could enjoy pursuing. While leading that seminar my col-
league and I asked, "How many of you have a longing to
be involved in some kind of activity that is close to your
heart, even though you may not be aware yet of what it
is?" Most of the hands in the room shot up! That question

had cut through layers of defenses, brushing aside any reserve, and had triggered a shared response. I was amazed at how deeply the wish to find "something" they could call their own, was embedded in the hearts and minds of these women. Everyone in the room suddenly seemed to be knit into a common bond of purpose and hope. We were all in agreement that we were serious about discovering and starting an independent venture each of us could find rewarding. Now all we had to do was figure out the best way to achieve that. Could we really shape a venture/interest around our own abilities, dreams, and goals?

I believed that we could. The capacity to direct such a venture is literally part of our own inherent capabilities and talents. We spent the remaining time in the seminar talking about what women could do to make their own dreams a reality.

The Act of Creating Your Life/Work

The role of creating an activity or entrepreneurial effort is a highly individual one in which you are actually giving structure and shape to something new. From that nothingness an enterprise of your own choosing gradually develops. Slowly, pieces fit together until the design becomes obvious and a new venture is born. There is a thrill in watching such a project take shape before your eyes. This is a process of not just one act, but of a whole series of acts.

Whether you realize it or not, you have likely experienced this type of creative process already. You may have planned an extensive trip, detail by detail, until that trip later became exactly what you hoped it to be; you may have planned a wedding that ultimately brought the deepest sense of happiness and joy, because you made it what you most wanted; you may have developed a hobby into the perfect leisure activity; you may have run for political office, until you achieved the victory of the campaign.

Whatever you did from your heart, and unreservedly put your hand to, became an expression of yourself, in your own image, and the visible creation of whatever you longed and planned for. Looking back you can see that like a work of art, the "creation" was authentic and bore the imprint of you, the designer. For me, the "bringing something out of nothing" is this book, the writing, the research, the beliefs, the convictions, even passions that I feel about its message and theme.

As you take an autobiographical journey through the years, you are going to realize what experiences and actions of yours were creative in nature, and how you can enjoy creative achievements in the future, successfully directing whatever you would like to do today. You will learn to think about skills you already have and to recognize the importance of what you've already done. *Your satisfying experiences, and the talents that were part of them, can be translated into a Life/Work project or venture that can be both enjoyable and long lasting.*

Directing a Meaningful Life/Work

You can design a creative activity such as Anne Morrow Lindbergh wrote about years ago. It can capture your heart and motivations, capitalize on the skills of your own hand, and be something that will continually refresh you. You are God's workmanship, created to do good works which God has prepared in advance for you to do!

The purpose of this book is to help you find out how your God-given talents can guide an activity/venture most suited for you. Let's start where you are and walk together through discovering your talents, deciding on the best ways to use them, and then starting whatever your enterprise might be. This should be an exciting journey!

As you begin, do you have any idea of the direction you want your life to take? Of the work you believe in and are good at? One that would meet the needs of others as well? Start by asking yourself three important questions:

• Who am I? (What abilities did God give me?)

• Where do I want to go? (What path will those abilities lead me down?)

• How will I get there? (What strategies will help me carry out my personal dreams and goals?)

At first glance you may think you know the answer to these questions: after all, they do concern you. But do you really know the strengths, resources, and dreams that reside within you? Could you explain them if you had the opportunity to do so? Understanding yourself is the key to any productive change. If you could do whatever you wanted to do, and go wherever you wanted to go, what would your life be like? Even more, how would you go about getting ready for your choice? Deciding the direction of your life is no easier than defining who you are. We have been pressured all our lives by numerous outside influences—by counselors, by "experts," by society and by parents to "just get a job," "go where the money is," or "stay home" and so on. Because direction is so often provided by forces outside of ourselves, we can easily fail to provide our own essential internal direction.

These unspoken questions are often in the hearts and minds of women. Although most women verbally acknowledge their presence, they can't give a clear, focused reply to the issues the questions raise. They desire answers, but don't know how to find them.

Unless you can clearly answer these questions, they may fester in your heart and mind, and may even be intimidating. However, they don't have to. You can find answers.

Discovering Who I Am

Begin by asking the first question, "Who am I?" Before you attempt to do anything in life, you need to know yourself better, and also to know how God made you. When you struggle with what you want to do with your life, you are really struggling to understand your own talents and capabilities. *What are the creative parts that make you who you are?*

- Your purpose and mission
- Your resources and abilities
- Your uniqueness

All are important because they make up your individuality. Your *purpose* or mission is what motivates you or what you are trying to accomplish; your resources assist you in the carrying out of that purpose, and in creating a project or work you care about. Your uniqueness is the sum of all that is you, not only your motivations and talents, but also the way you express yourself, your style, and personality. It is what makes you different from everyone else, the stamp on everything you do.

Defining who you are—your purposes, creativity, personal resources and uniqueness—can best be done by doing a complete inventory and stock-taking of yourself, and by carefully looking at each of these creative parts one at a time, in this chapter and in chapters 3 and 4.

Guidance consultants suggest that we can learn about ourselves by reviewing our lives and by looking for a common thread that runs throughout all we have done. Businessman-counselor Arthur Miller and educator Ralph T. Mattson, in *Finding a Job You Could Love,*[1] state that each person carries out his or her God-given motivations and abilities in a very particular way. What a person does comes from an individual will and design. They suggest that if we examine what a person freely wills to do—those actions which result in personal satisfaction—we can discover a pattern that has been there all along. Many psychologists concur that we are born with that pattern. You can ask God to reveal the purposes He has for your life, purposes that are written into your very being.

What is your purpose? Do you have one? A lack of defined purpose could be causing an indifference or lethargy in your life now, or it could be the reason you feel such a strong desire to find a new activity. It doesn't matter if you haven't defined a clear purpose yet, as long as you understand the necessity of having one.

Why is having a sense of purpose so important? In addition to providing impetus and commitment for your efforts, finding a goal or mission you can believe in can also provide the motivation to excel in life. Purposeful living gives meaning to all you do.

A definite purpose can also mean the difference between a halfhearted effort and one achieved with excellence. You will never be motivated to wholeheartedly perform a task, do a job, offer a service, or create a product until you find that which engages your heart, as well as your hand, tapping the special motivations and skills God has placed in you.

Where Is Your Heart? What Do You Find Exciting?

To discover a purpose that will motivate you, think about those times past and present when you really enjoyed what you were doing, and were naturally motivated. Your purposes or heart experiences may have been expressed in tasks you did in the home, in favorite hobbies, in work, or in special interests you pursued. Some of your happiest times may have been in your childhood or during volunteer activities in community or church. To capture that kind of satisfaction again, you need to tap whatever motivated you before, and to create a new enterprise based on what is most important to you.

Let's hear one woman describe how she found a purpose she believed in and incorporated it in an enterprise of her own choosing. Finding a sense of purpose gave Randi the courage and the go-ahead to create an activity she finds of great value to her. Today she conducts international self-management and growth seminars and is very much in demand, but it wasn't always that way.

Randi's Story

I had just gone through a personal crisis in my life because of divorce, and that crisis and being on my own with a child, caused me to start thinking anew about myself. I suddenly had a real need to find out who I was, what my strengths were, and what I could do. I had a career before as a sales distributor and representative for a line of imported ski clothing, but now I had an intense desire to redefine and to make sense of all that I was, or of the little that I was. I knew I would have to find some kind of work that could both support me and be a career I would enjoy.

As I started to look at life with new eyes, I began to understand that I was responsible for my own life. I also began a deeper search for meaning.

I discovered that my knowledge and acceptance of myself was very limited—but I also knew I had achieved many results so far and that must count for something. In my earlier career, and even later, I spent a lot of time on planes traveling across the ocean to Europe, and spent much of that time talking with other travelers. Those conversations proved to be a research field and a sounding board for me. I became more aware that most people either thought they had to be all things, and therefore always felt discouraged because they weren't, or did not understand that they too were limited, and only had to be themselves.

I often reassured myself and my travel companions that we did not need to be able to do everything. God did not make us to be all things. I noticed people were responding to our little talks, and expressing their thanks to me for being of help to them. I also noticed this subject always aroused my deepest concerns.

My calling was born! I decided I wanted to do something that could show others, limited as we all might be, that our own capabilities are all that matter. We only have to be who we are. I felt a strong desire to give something back to the world. This was where my heart was. However, I didn't know where my journey was taking me. I had big financial responsibilities and was in charge of my own home and my own life—for better or for worse—but my own past hurt and desire for growth were so consuming that if I had not eventually turned these concerns and interests into a business, I would have been in greater need both emotionally and economically.

I found myself involved next in doing a whole inventory of my life and my resources to see how I could use them in some kind of career or business. I knew the thrust of that effort would be to help people manage their own lives (which I was undertaking now partly out of desperation and partly out of need) and to help them grow and use their own natural abilities. In order to give added structure and assistance to what I was doing, I called on close friends, business friends, and on executives. I hired a career counselor and employed the help of a psychologist to help me organize my thoughts and my business professionally. By one year later I had designed a Personal Management Tool Kit and had started giving seminars in a friend's home—I was off and running!

Today I am able to market these seminars to industry . . . and I am happy to say that there have been deep and lasting results. Others have changed. I have changed. I have absolutely no regrets about the time and the struggles that enabled me to do what I am now doing. I will say, however, that when I was in the middle of these changes and new directions, I felt like giving up on making my life come together—there were just so many challenges. To me it was not a luxury to work and be self-supporting—I really had no choice.

I guess all of us want easy answers. But I would say to women: You have the resources or the dreams to do what you really would like to do. I can say I am truly in love with life now, and I hope you will be able to say that too.

Randi's search led her to find her own purpose by helping others to find theirs. Her seminars are always filled, affirming her Life/Work choice.

History's greats have acknowledged this significance of purpose. The Hall of Fame for them was not getting a gold medal, being a movie star, seeing their pictures in the paper, or receiving accolades. Their reward came from adherence to a worthy purpose. Helen Keller expressed it so well: "Many persons have a wrong idea of what constitutes true happiness. It is not attained through self-gratification, but through fidelity to a worthy purpose."[2]

As you think over your life, recall when you were motivated as Randi was, and engaged in something you felt especially good about. These activities and experiences will be characterized by the natural enthusiasm, motivation, and strength of purpose you brought to them. Try to identify the elements of your motivational pattern.

For example, as I looked back over my own life, I realized that I had often been involved in affirming others. I remember as a young child feeling bad for school friends who were not happy, or who didn't believe in themselves. I often wanted to encourage others to see their uniqueness and potential. Many times they didn't realize their value and sold themselves short.

Years later in business, I began to realize that I basically enjoyed the same thing, that is, I had an interest in understanding what a business had the potential to become. These personal motivations seem to have always been present. I decided to make them part of the purpose of another entrepreneurial effort, the writing of this book.

As you look at what motivates you, do you see a recurring pattern? Were you always improving, motivating, confronting, affirming, perfecting, pioneering, leading, constructing, serving, teaching, helping, comforting, analyzing, creating . . . ?

Richard Nelson Bolles, author of *What Color Is Your Parachute?* has stated that your deepest purpose is to identify the core of your life, that constant thread that persists through all the changing world around you.[3] He too claims you can see a pattern and consistency, as you look over your past rewarding achievements. These experiences can be helpful in showing the choices you can have for your life. Again your vision is enlarged.

My Experience/Motivation Chart

List meaningful experiences you have had through the years. Then identify the pattern of constancy of purpose and motivation that may have been present in each one.

My Meaningful Experiences
(Record the motivation present in most of your activities)

My Motivations in Each Experience

Experience 1.
(This could have been a hobby.)

Motivations for Experience 1.
(What motivated you in your hobby?)

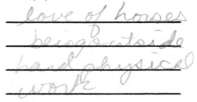

getting a horse,

love of horses
being outside
hard physical
work

Experience 2.
(This could have been a volunteer activity.)

Motivations for Experience 2.
(What motivated you to pursue this activity?)

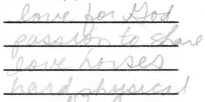

working at Miracle Ranch

love for God
passion to share
love horses
hard physical
work

Experience 3.
(This could have been a church-related office or job.)

Motivations for Experience 3.
(Why did you do this job?)

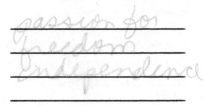

Moving out

passion for
freedom
independence

Experience 4.
(This could have been work-related.)

Getting job at Swedish

Motivations for Experience 4.
(Why did you pursue this work?)

love wk. that takes patience & skill in wkng with people

Experience 5.
(This could have been home-related.)

Getting married & starting family

Motivations for Experience 5.
(What did you most enjoy doing in your home?)

Creating an atmosphere of peace & comfort, an oasis in the world

Experience 6.
(This could have been school-related.)

Coming home to be at home mom

Motivations for Experience 6.
(What did you like about this activity?)

I'm training her, I know where she is. to protect her & love her.

Review what you have written, looking for similarities in your recorded experiences and motivations.

Now, see if you can express your life's motivational thrust in a concise purpose statement.

As you begin any new venture, it is crucially important that your basic motivations be a part of it. They can make all the difference in the direction and success of your Life/Work.

Challenge

My Purpose/Motivation Statement

Making possible the
impossible with hard phy.
work ... passion for
peace.

Test this statement. Does it really excite you and make you want to do something about it? If not, you'll need to take a closer look at what motivates you, and refine your purpose and mission.

It will be the strength of your purpose that will sustain you when you are faced with the struggles or fears of directing your own life and creative work. That purpose will provide meaning and staying power when others wonder how you keep on going. It is the secret to not quitting.

It is now time to look at the next creative part that encompasses who you are, your resources and strengths. Anne Lindbergh wrote, "Every woman must find her true center alone." You are going to be taking a closer look at that center, which represents your core of talents and your true self.

Where Is Your Hand? What Have You Done Well?

As you have looked at your heart motivations, now you will look at your hand—the talents that are evident in many of your experiences and accomplishments. What are the talents God has given you? His desire is that those talents be used, and that you be filled "with the knowledge of His will through all spiritual wisdom and understanding . . . bearing fruit in every good work, growing in the knowledge of God" (Colossians 1:9-10). We see that God wants your work to be successful and to bear fruit. He is a partner in your labors, and wants you to have knowledge of His will for your life. You best perceive God's will when you discern your own gifts. That will is written into your own being.

In reviewing your life and achievements and successes of varying magnitude, searching for your resources and talents, not all of your experiences need be documented. The ones of significance are those in which you were most yourself. There is a way to discover when those experiences occurred in your life and to make your inventorying a bit easier.

Psychologists call such events "peak experiences." By definition these "identity experiences" are distinguished by peak motivation, peak performance, and satisfaction. According to the late Abraham Maslow, a psychologist renowned for his study of self-actualization, these experiences are characterized by times when:

• You felt more integrated, more whole.

• You had a feeling of oneness with what you were doing, to the point of being unaware of yourself. (An artist caught up in his painting.)

• You performed with ease, perhaps so easily that you even took for granted what you were doing.

• You had a feeling of being in control, of being the creative center of your own activities and perceptions.

• You were spontaneous, less inhibited by fears and therefore more creative; you acted not out of any end purpose other than that of what you were doing.

• You may have been surprised by joy, both before and after, almost an "I don't deserve this" attitude.[4]

Can you recall when you felt these elements were present? *Don't overlook achievements you may have taken for granted.* For example, I know a woman who is always organizing everything and everyone. She does a great job, but when she is complimented, she will say, "Don't you do this too?" Her strengths are so natural to her that she makes the mistake of assuming everyone has them; she has a hard time believing her resources are "special." Until she does, she will not be in a position to really capitalize on her organizational skills.

Many of us overlook the obvious and discount our own

abilities. What is easy for us is such a part of us that we don't recognize the skills we use.

Your identity experiences could be evidenced in anything from hobbies you pursued, to skills or talents you used in the home or in church or other organizations, to volunteer work you have done, or to activities you found yourself often seeking and doing. Your achievements also may be evident in relationships you have had with peers, or in school or employment experiences. Hidden in so many of these personal events are nuggest of truth about yourself—mainly *why* you always did what you did, and *how* you did it.

My Most Satisfying Experiences

Make a list of the achievements and successes in which you used your talents in ways that were personally rewarding or gratifying.

1. I was self-motivated and used my own abilities when:

There was a stack of stuff no one wanted to finish & I did it w/o being asked.

2. I had an experience I was absorbed in when:

ride horses
walk
counselling w/ Word

3. I had an experience where I said, "This is really me" when:

at 35 listen to
the lesson

4. I had an experience that came easily because it called on my best strengths when:

helping Donna & Sheila

5. I had an experience where I took charge when:

Cheryls kids

6. I sought out a particular experience because it was creative and I simply enjoyed doing it when:

Decorating bathroom

7. I experienced joy in helping others when:

_____

_____

_____

_____

_____

Before we go any further, let's talk to a woman who looked at her own experiences and spotted some common threads. She discovered her talents and interests and turned them into an activity that could embrace them.

Kay's Story

I was in my thirties, mother of two, when the realization came to me that I had half of my life still to live, and I wasn't sure what I was going to do with it. It was a startling thought—there would be no more babies, no more work around the home that would consume me day and night. I started looking for something else—but I wasn't sure where to go or what to do. I wanted to do 'something' that was fulfilling to me and to society. I had been a fairly fortunate person in life, and I felt a strong responsibility to give something back. I did not want to run out and get a high paying job, or to spend my time at the country club. . . . Whatever I did must have meaning to me personally, and to others.

My credentials at that time were minimal. Sixteen years earlier I had two years at Skidmore College, and I felt a need to go back to school and get even further education, retraining myself to do something new. I decided to apply to Wellesley College in my early forties, and was so thrilled when I was accepted and invited to come. It was like someone else saying to me, 'We think you can do it.' I enrolled and spent four years at Wellesley, taking a partial work load at first, mainly because I had to consider other things such as my home, the financial burden of attending school, and my own initial fears that I could handle school again. I wanted to approach my new goals very carefully.

School proved to be a good thing for me. I started to get the affirmation from it and from other students that I could do what I had chosen to do. Women need that, we all need an occasional pat on the back. I finally graduated from school (everyone thought I was turning into a perennial student!) and began to think about going on to graduate school. I had become more and more aware of my interest in history and decided to turn an avocation into a vocation. I applied to Boston University for a master's degree in historical preservation. Preserving the beauty and architecture of some of our country's best buildings and best designs was something that really motivated me and concerned me. It was exciting to turn that desire into an activity that I could find satisfying. For two more years I would be a student again! But I had a focused goal in mind, a purpose, and something I specifically was aiming for.

After completing my degree, I started my own venture called Preservation Plus, doing free lance appraising, and also advising on the refurbishing of historic properties. I really enjoy what I am doing, and I feel it was worth every single day that I had to put into making it what it now is.

You too want to employ the resources and skills that were part of your more rewarding experiences and interests. You are continuing to look for the common thread of talents that keep appearing in your activities and in your life.

Try to better understand the different abilities and skills

you have, and how they have often been used. If the snow-flake has its own design, you can be sure God has placed a unique blueprint or design within your own nature. God can help reveal that pattern of talents to you. It has likely been demonstrated in your personal interests and hobbies. It may revolve around skills you have in decorating, in architecture, in handling fabrics and design, in crafts, in speaking or writing, in computers, in cooking, in sociology or theology and so on. With a little imagination and insight, these personal resources can be the core or foundation for the new activity you are planning. Any "work," whether leisure or occupational, can be used to help direct a new venture or enterprising effort.

My Achievement/Talent Chart

List again your achievement experiences, but this time fill in the talents that were part of each. You may also think of experiences that escaped your attention before.

My Satisfying Achievement Experiences
(As recorded earlier, or added to.)
Experience 1.
(Could have been a hobby.)

The Talents I Used in Them

Talents for Experience 1.

_____

_____

_____

_____

_____

_____

Experience 2.
(Could have been work-related.)

Talents for Experience 2.

_____

_____persistence____

_____

_____teaching____

_____

_____

Experience 3.
(Could have been a childhood experience.)

_____

_____

_____

_____

Talents for Experience 3.

people skills
patience
persistence
typing

Experience 4.
(Could have been a volunteer activity.)

_____

_____

_____

_____

Talents for Experience 4.

_____

_____

_____

_____

Experience 5.
(Could have related to being a homemaker.)

_____

_____

_____

_____

Talents for Experience 5.

creativity
patience
persistence

Experience 6.
(Could have related to an organization, a group experience, or a church activity.)

_____

_____

_____

_____

Talents for Experience 6.

_____

_____

_____

_____

As you study your list of achievements pay close attention to the details of each. Can you see common points? For instance, which talents were you frequently using, and what were you putting your "hand" to? You will find if you have chosen a purpose-mission that really motivates you, your talents will be employed in the carrying out of that mission.

Talents Present in My Achievement Experiences

Write a descriptive statement that you think best expresses the abilities you drew on in your more gratifying achievements in life.

Summarize the abilities and talents you usually used that could be incorporated in an activity or Life/Work.

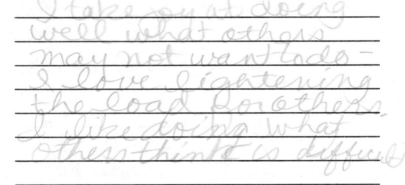

I take joy at doing well what others may not want to do — I love lightening the load for others. I like doing what others think is difficult.

Take a thorough look at all you've done, because those unnoticed or undramatic moments are the ones you are most apt to take for granted. You may be too busy looking for the spectacular or for what society encourages you to emulate.

Are you finding your natural resources? Your transferable skills can be some of your best assets, as you realize the possibilities they offer. I know a woman who took her knitting skills and turned them into a custom design business, taking orders for unique sweaters and other items of clothing. Another woman recognized her skills of management and organization; after years of nursing, she applied for a management position in a large hospital. Yet another woman, who thought she could sell anything (as her friends often told her) and liked fashion, formed an enterprise in which she would sell imported jewelry from Europe. All these women appreciated abilities which could be used in a new setting.

As you look at your major motivation and abilities, think of how they can help shape an entrepreneurial activity or endeavor that you can develop as a Life/Work. For example, if your interests and skills have been in serving and helping people, you can design an activity that accomplishes this.

Let's talk to another woman who faced the challenge of finding her innate abilities and of drawing on her past and present experiences to create a venture of her own. You can observe how Carol approached her skills and interests and turned them into something that gives her great pleasure.

Carol has a family, but she also desired to do other things with her life. She has started doing them, very successfully, but let her speak for herself.

Carol's Story
My father always said, 'Go into teaching.' He felt the big world wasn't safe, and certainly not ready, at that time, for a woman who wanted to step into the world of business. I followed his advice and eventually got married.

I had a whole life ahead of me, but at age twenty-seven a feeling of discontentment began to sweep over me. I didn't recognize what this discontent was about, but felt that it was probably due to a lack of stimulation in my life. I knew the time was soon coming when my children would not need me so much. I did enjoy them and my home, and never felt held down by them—it is such a short time in one's life that one has them—but I needed something more stimulating in my life than to have my husband come home and ask me either what groceries I bought, or how I 'spent' my day. I considered it a personal affront, although he was not to blame.

It's funny. All I wanted when I was younger was to have a family, and only after I had it all did I feel that something was missing, and that it was not enough. I realized that by the time I was forty-four my youngest child would be away at school; what was I going to do with my remaining years?

As a side interest I began to be involved in decorating, and noticed that I had the abilities to be good at it. It started as a hobby, but I started to take it more seriously. I got up the courage and enrolled in a design course in Boston, while continuing to find I really enjoyed my new-found pursuits. After completing the course I became more and more involved in doing small decorating jobs, and the success with each one gave me the confidence to go on to the next. Fortunately I was able to structure my time around the responsibilities of my home, and work at my business slowly, so I never felt that my family was losing out or being short-changed.

As the children got even older, and my time became freer, my business really grew. Perhaps I had luck on my side, because much of what I did was not really planned—it just seemed to take off. Now, however, I am treating my business very "professionally." I am serious about it, and it is something I enjoy.

Initially, though, it was very hard to go back to school for training—there were no assurances that the time and effort I put in would pay off—and being older made it seem double the effort. I wondered if I could really take on the challenges I was choosing. Now I am so glad that I did.

As you create the activity that could be ideal for you, part of your task is deciding what is "ideal" — the activity, the setting, the involvement level that appeals to you most. You may want to design something that is entrepreneurial in character or is self-directed, but isn't really a business. Or, you may choose to start a business.

You may also need to ask yourself whether you should take steps such as Kay and Carol did — going back to school, enrolling in a course, reading all you can on a subject, or studying what others with similar interests and abilities as yours have done. It will depend on your plans. When you have a better idea of what you want to do, you can determine if a broadening of your abilities and background is needed.

What Is Your Trademark? Finding Your Own Uniqueness

You are at the point in your journey of discovering the third creative part of who you are, your own uniqueness — the motivations, abilities, style that are yours. Women have often found it difficult to talk about their uniqueness, or even worse, have denied it. You should know why you are special and understand how that "specialness" can be expressed in your work or in any creative effort you undertake. You are God's creation, and as Ethel Waters said, "God don't make no mistakes."

Your challenge is to not only understand what makes you unique, but also to understand how you can express that uniqueness, no matter what it is, in whatever you do. You have a personal way of carrying out your tasks and expressing yourself that is different from others. This is your blueprint of who you are.

Let's meet Fran, a woman who owns and manages a temporary help agency that matches people with jobs requiring short-term assistance, and see how she came to use her own uniqueness in her life and in her work. Fran is someone who is not afraid to let her uniqueness show through, and to openly express it. She has made it an asset and not a liability.

Fran's Story

The phone rang. It was my husband, calling from the office, our office, our business. . . . "Would you consider coming back into the business? I need you. . . ." Those are magic words—need me? Well, I thought it might be time to get busy again. Children are leaving, house is emptying and I do need to grow and get out of my nest. I'm thinking to myself, well, in a world where people need people, I do feel that I have a lot to give and can help people. That's our business, helping people, in the temporary placement division as well as the permanent placement division of our corporation.

At this point in my life I needed to do something useful that would enable me to benefit myself, and more than that, hopefully help others.

It's difficult to grow! It hurts. Sometimes we say, "Why do I need to go through this? Wouldn't it be better just to take life easy?" The answer, of course, is "No!" First of all, I enjoy people, and in helping people I get the benefit, as well as they.

Growing also means stretching—trying new things and even failing—if we're not prepared to fail, then we're not prepared to grow.

Growing. Also there is FAITH. Without faith in one's ability and uniqueness, and faith in God, we're not even going to try. There have been many instances where I have dared to stretch and trust my faith that God would help solve a specific problem. One day—it was a very busy, telephone-ringing-off-the-hook day—one of my clients needed three good people immediately—tomorrow. I didn't have them. Quickly I said, 'God, You've got to help me again. I really need these people and I don't have them. And oh, by the way, I need them in half an hour!' Stretching your faith? Yes. Well, of course, I got the three people—sent them to work, and incidentally, the order was filled in thirty minutes!

Faith—uniqueness of one's ability, stretching, hurting and, yes, even at times crying—means growing, and growing is a benefit, a benefit to everyone, but they can't be separated. They are individual and yet together. What is my dream? To continue in an upward path, to dig down for those resources that God provides in us all, to see them bubble to the surface and burst into joy—there's nothing more satisfying than improving one's self and in doing so, helping other people to grow and improve.

It is obvious Fran has many special things about her, not the least of which is a hearty spirit, a strong faith, and belief in herself. It is also obvious that she expresses that uniqueness in her daily activities, and that others are directly benefiting from it.

Can you express your uniqueness in your own venture or Life/Work, as Fran is doing? Study again your achievement charts that record what motivates you and what talents and resources you have used in your more satisfying experiences. What do you see that is different about you and how you do what you do? For instance, *how* did you find yourself implementing your purposes and using your abilities in involvements that were really "you"? It is in the "doing" that your uniqueness will be most discernible.

Your style, personality, beliefs, and values can be the extra that you bring to your work and creative activities. A small difference can be turned into a big difference, *if* you understand what is special about you from the very beginning. Do you have an unusual way or gift with people, or a unique way of doing things? Are you a natural leader? Do you desire to be a role model for others? Do you have a high set of standards? Or a good sense of humor? Think of how those traits can be part of an effort or enterprise, the stamp that will also make it different.

Write a short paragraph stating the uniqueness you can incorporate in your Life/Work:

My Uniqueness

_____

_____

_____

_____

_____

Transfer all you have recorded in this chapter to your Life/Work Chart.

As you more and more see that you are God's handiwork and have been designed with special gifts and a built-in motivation to use those gifts, that understanding can provide the faith to believe that God has special plans for you, "good works which He has prepared in advance." The future is filled with possibilities. These exercises should have dissolved any lingering doubts about whether or not this is a journey you truly want, or have the courage to take. You will likely find yourself unable to turn back, if for no other reason than to find out what lies ahead.

MY LIFE/WORK CHART

(Transferred from what you recorded earlier.)
I. Who Am I?

This is to be determined by my own nature and the "pattern" God gave me.

A. My purpose/mission (behind my actions; the motivational pattern seemingly behind all I do and that is present in my "heart" experiences).

My purpose (that I could incorporate in an activity) is:

_____

_____

_____

_____

B. My resources, my hands-on experiences and talents (that can assist me in carrying out my purpose and in building an activity of value and worth) are:

_____

_____

_____

_____

C. My uniqueness (the sum of my parts and *how* I put them to use).

_____

_____

_____

_____

II. Where Do I Want To Go? (to be filled in later)

Chapter Three

Dreaming To Find Your Direction

Delight yourself in the Lord and He will give you the
desires of your heart.

Psalm 37:4

You have taken a look at yourself and have begun to get an
idea of what motivates you and what talents are your best
strengths. That vision of yourself may have helped you
gain a better glimpse of what you could do, or who you can
become.

What kind of a future can you envision? What do you
dream of doing? What is closest to your heart? It is important to know what you want for your life, and to understand how God might be directing you. What would inspire
you enough to devote your time and energies to achieving
it? If you aren't sure, finding out will be an inspiring and
interesting task.

At this point, you're ready to ask the second question,
"WHERE DO I WANT TO GO?"

In 1989, *Christianity Today* asked its readers which
religious questions were of most interest to them. Sixty-
two percent responded, "Does God have a plan for my life,
and am I living it?"[1] Considering that the average age of
their reader is forty, this was surprising. Mid-life people, as
well as young people, are seeking guidance for their lives
and wondering how to find it.

To discover a sense of direction for your own life, look

Discovering
Where I Want To Go

again at your resources as recorded on your chart, and ask, "What is my core of abilities that I can lead with? What way of life or activity does the pattern of my own abilities and interests indicate?" As you let your design of talents point the way, and as you follow your heart's desire, a path toward your life's "work" should begin to become evident. Within the demand character of your own nature you will find some guides.

As you examine the resources at your disposal, ask yourself, "What do I see myself doing and becoming to fulfill my potential?" That vision can be transformed into specific goals that express what you want to achieve and to become. As you then surrender those dreams and goals to God, He can make even crooked paths straighten out before you. What seemed impossible becomes possible. God has promised to provide guidance and help for you. "Trust in the Lord with all your heart and lean not unto your own understanding; in all your ways acknowledge Him, and He will make your paths straight (Proverbs 3:5-6).

Women living in the 1990s need to engage in some individual and collective dreaming to capture a higher and better vision of life and work. It is the substance, not the size, of the vision that counts. One can't help but wonder what could happen if more and more women across our land began to dream, particularly women who allowed God to dream and to create through them.

There could be an expansion of freedom, of what it means to be *woman*, in every sense of the word—homemaker, wife, mother, and creator/partner with God. Our own households would praise us as well as our own works. We would be like the woman described in Proverbs 31.

> She considers a field, and buys it: out of her earnings she plants a vineyard. She sets about her work vigorously; her arms are strong for her tasks. She sees that her trading is profitable. . . . She opens her arms to the poor and extends her hands to the needy. . . . She makes linen garments and sells them, and supplies the merchants with sashes. . . . She watches over the affairs of her household and does not eat of the bread of idleness. . . . Give her the reward she has earned, and let her works bring her praise at the city gate.

What a woman this was, combining many different entreprenuerial activities and work in the home! The dreaming you will do is not pie-in-the-sky, lacking connection with reality. Rather, it is rooted in your own aspirations and abilities, and in the desires God plants within you. Your dreams can show you what you are capable of doing. They lift your sights and your belief in yourself.

But your dreams need to be realistic and evidence the balance that your life requires. You no longer have to dream of "having it all," or of being all things to all people, for this was a misconception and burden placed on us by outside societal influences. Women who haven't followed such cultural mandates have been made to feel "inadequate." Rather, you can dream instead of what is best for you. Being Superwoman is "out." Some women almost killed themselves trying so hard to please or to do. God doesn't call you to be a workaholic, or to make trade-offs that bring harm to yourself or to others.

Where Do I Want To Go?

The best way to discover your dream of achievement is to separate your stronger desires from your lesser ones, and so to find what is most important to you. In fact it has been said that discovery of your soul's sincere desires, those that come from deep within *you*, is the only way to test your true life purposes. Before you decide on a dream that is realistic and authentic for you, let's hear other women describe their dreams.

Mary lives in the Midwest with her husband and their four older children. She married at twenty-nine, and at age fifty-five, much of her time is still spent taking care of her family and tending to their needs. However, Mary has started to think about her life and about new dreams she has.

Mary's Story

On my journey through life I feel like I have done everything backward. After becoming a mother for the last time at age thirty-seven, when most of my friends' children were already halfway grown up, I really didn't have the time to think a lot about the future. In fact it was a pleasure and thrill for me to go to the supermarket alone!

I can't yet separate myself from the rest of the family, although I know it's coming soon. When all the kids have gone off to college or work and Bob and I are all alone, I am not even sure what we will talk about. For the past nineteen years it has been, "I'll call you at 6 o'clock" or "Leave me a note on the kitchen table." My journey so far has been filled with other people.

In the future I would like to find something to do that would involve just me. I would like to get to the point where I feel relaxed and comfortable enough to put my thoughts and wishes together and write a column for a local newspaper or magazine. Perhaps this is wishful thinking—I know there are three million column writers out there who are probably better at writing than I, but still I would like to try. I truly wish I had a gift for communication—I would be very happy with myself and my life if I could communicate much better with my husband, my friends, my children, my relatives, God, the schools, and my dog. Having already tried nursing for several years before marrying, I am not interested in that anymore. I am ready to try new things. In the meantime, I hope I can accept my life gracefully, no matter what state it is in, or I am in. I want to constantly grow and expose myself to new ideas.

My daughter, Sheri, is an attractive married woman who just turned thirty. In the past she combined being a wife and running a fashion-color business that helped women to find their best style, image, and dressing. But Sheri's life is changing. She is taking a look at herself and her future with a new commitment.

Sheri did not complete college, but left to start her business and career. Finishing her schooling has meant a lot to her. She would also like to be involved in helping people with their personal needs and struggles. This sounds rewarding and worthwhile, but Sheri has her own frustrations and fears, along with her dreams. She puts it this way:

Sheri's Story
I dropped out of college since I didn't have any interest in finishing at that time. I started a small business venture whose purpose was to help women enhance their physical appearance, to improve how they looked and felt. Through that experience I discovered I enjoyed working with people and speaking to groups

and I gained confidence in being able to deal with people. For the first time I felt that my life was significant, and that I had gifts and talents that I could use in meaningful ways.

Now, however, I desire to be involved in some form of family and marriage counseling or social work with the homeless, and to help others with more than just their outward appearance. I realize that I need to complete my education to carry out that dream.

It will take time to finish the necessary schooling, but I know it will be worth it. One thought that has strengthened me in pursuing my dream is something a former teacher shared with a class I once had. He told us the career we choose should be one that we enjoy so much that we would feel miserable doing anything else. He said if we didn't have passion for what we were choosing, we shouldn't be involved in it. His statement has given me the determination to pursue my dream.

It is frustrating, though, to think of completing my education when I consider my biological clock will be saying, 'If you want to have children, you'd better have them soon.'

But I do believe in the long run I will be more fulfilled than if I had settled for something that would have been safe and expedient. I do not want to arrive at midlife and have regrets about what I could have done. I see so many people suffering through that. I want to eventually have something of my own, because my whole life has been a piece of everyone else.

The biggest challenge I now face is to live each day rather than thinking my life will begin when I achieve my dreams.

Many of Sheri's dreams have already come true, as she has married an outstanding young man named Keith, and has since gone back to school and achieved an excellence unmatched before. She will have graduated from college by the time you read this book, and will decide then if more study is needed to pursue her other interests. I am very proud of Sheri, and I know God is going to use her in some really special ways.

Dreaming with Variables

Take out your Life/Work Chart and look at what you have already discovered about yourself. What can you see yourself doing, as you consider your abilities? Ask God to show you the dream that could best fulfill the talents He has given you. The dream He has for you will probably be bigger than you are and allow you to touch other people's lives.

Let's do a dreaming exercise. Pick a place of solitude where you will be undisturbed; close your eyes, relax, and picture yourself using your abilities and motivations in as many ways as possible. In a meditative or contemplative mood, hold quietly before you a vision of achievement. For the time being, shut out any negative thoughts, and any reasons why an idea will not work.

Keep "trying your dreams on," sifting them through your intuitive processes. Don't hold back. This is not the time to let logic get in the way. Dreams can be easily sabotaged just as they are being born, especially if your "logic" claims that they won't work.

The variables you can creatively dream about are *why*, *what*, *how*, and *where*.

● *Why* you would be doing a certain activity—the strong motivations you would be tapping.

● *What* you would be doing as you use your best talents and strengths.

● *How* you would be carrying out your activity—the uniqueness of style you bring to all you do.

● *Where* you would be performing it.

By moving these variables around, you can change both the activity and the setting. Pay attention to the images that appear in your mind and to their details. Are you imagining an independent project? A volunteer activity? Are you involved in starting a business? What talents are employed? Where are you? Are you working alone or with others? Is this something you love to do? Stretch your mind and imagination until you focus on a dream that particularly seems to excite you.

As I went through my own dreaming process, I discovered the desire to help women who were concerned with the same things I am, namely, discovering ways to use our abilities, finding worthwhile activities, and knowing God's will. I entertained a number of possibilities to accomplish this—being a consultant to women in business; giving entrepreneur seminars for women; helping women find new ways of creative expression; writing and speaking on how women are meeting their own personal needs while fulfilling their God-given talents; doing something in the media, i.e., writing or collaborating on a documentary film or docudrama on stories of women's desires to use the full range of their abilities and how they are responding to that challenge. It was fun "to try out" as many dreams as I could think of, everything from the sublime to the ridiculous.

Eventually my dreams began to take shape, and so will yours. I began to feel that I did not want to be engaged in business. There went the consultant idea and some others. After much trial and error, I realized all our lives need moments of inspiration to help get us through our days and tasks. Therefore I wanted my own activity to include an inspirational as well as a practical emphasis.

Even though I was using my own resources in all of my dreams, I discovered that the dreams which appealed to me the most included my strongest priorities and motivations. That was a quite a revelation. *How* I used my resources, the process, context and setting, was as important to me as *what* I did. This book became the way I chose to carry out my own dreams and goals. It was not the path I logically would have picked, but it was the one that would not let me go.

The dream that just "clicks," or grabs you and will not let go, should give you a feeling of peace. It should motivate you to want to act upon it. That dream should make you feel very centered; you keep coming back to it, even if it isn't the one you would first have chosen. Your dream fits, everything falls into place as you think about it. When you move away from this dream, things seem wrong. Your motivation disappears.

If God has something special for you, you have a knowledge of it inside you which causes you not to be satisfied with anything else. The thing to do is to find out what God's plan is. When the right door appears and you open it, you will "know" it is right.

Now identify the dream that excites you most and that indicates where you want to go. List as much about it as you can.

My Dream—The Desire of My Heart

Does this motivating dream represent your strongest desires? (These are the desires that come from within you, and are not desires based on external reasons to achieve— such as money, trends in society, advice of friends.) A vision or dream from God will allow you to get a glimpse of your potential. That potential may surprise you.

Record the dream that represents what you would most "desire" to see fulfilled in your future, if you feel that dream is right for you.

II. Where Do I Want To Go?

This means setting my course, by letting the pattern of my God-given abilities and talents set my direction and path.

A. My creative dreaming reveals that I would like to do or become:

_____

_____

_____

_____

_____

_____

Congratulations on discovering a dream and daring to put it in writing! This is the first step to developing your talents, and the vision or plans God has for those talents.

Are you afraid your dreams and desires might not come true? As you "delight yourself in the Lord, He will give you the desires of your heart." That is a promise, conditioned only by your putting God first. In fact, this is but one of the "very great and precious promises" God has given you.

Hannah Whitall Smith, writing in *The Christian's Secret of a Happy Life*, a book first published in 1870, says that faith is "simply believing God. . . . As sight is only seeing, so faith is only believing. . . . The virtue does not lie in your believing, but in the thing you believe. I beg of you to recognize, then, the extreme simplicity of faith; namely, that it is nothing more nor less than just believing God when He says He either has done something for us, or will do it; and then trusting Him to keep His word."[2]

There is a feeling of exhilaration in daring to dream dreams you might never have dreamed before. Yet even if you have found a dream worth going after, the road ahead may seem overwhelming to you. I have often discovered that the very things I spent my life saying I could never do, later proved to be surprisingly not only something I could do, but enjoyed doing.

In my case, I spent years somewhat in awe of women who seemed to have a business acumen. I felt I did not have that type of mind. It wasn't until I made the decision to sit in on the board meetings of our primary business, a national label company, that I began to get an indication of what managing a business was all about. It was interesting in those meetings to listen to ideas as they were discussed and to see how decisions were made. It seemed that common sense resolved much of what had to be done. Business, as a result, became less of a mystery and more a matter of trying to think carefully and use good judgment. That understanding gave me the confidence to be involved in my own business activities, and to stop placing unnecessary limitations on myself.

Dreams Become Goals

Catherine Marshall had dreams of her own to be tested. She was married to Peter Marshall, the famed chaplain to the United States Senate. Because of his position, she had more than her share of "glory," as the world would call it. She was anxious, however, to stretch her own talents. While on a retreat at an inn in the Valley of Virginia, she sought for answers to her own search for fuller use of her abilities. Catherine Marshall had taken along Glenn Clark's *I Will Lift Up Mine Eyes*. This little book, written in 1938, caused her to think back over her childhood and her life. Who had she been? What had she dreamed of in earlier years? Suddenly she saw herself as a young girl, "sitting with her back against an ancient locust tree, gazing dreamily . . . there I conceived the idea of being a writer."[3] Her desire to be a writer was still there! She put her desires on paper, being as specific as possible, and submitted them to a series of hurdles or tests, to see whether her dreams were true to her own nature and therefore requests that she felt she had a right to make of God. She asked herself if her dreams would fulfill her particular talents, temperament, and emotional needs, and finally concluded they would. The rest is history. Catherine Marshall went on to write not one but many books and was best known for her beloved, *A Man Called Peter*, a book eventually turned into a movie. Even though she is gone, and missed, her creative contributions are still with us.

If our dreams are to come true, we will need to let them set our goals. Those goals will be the indication of what we want to do and to become. Goal-setting, unfortunately, is not a job many of us are inclined to do or enjoy. Odd, isn't it, that successful businesses don't leave their future to happenstance but establish goals to guarantee their future will be the one they desire, while we live with little thought about our own future. We keep putting in one day after another, and another, and another, hoping everything will "turn out all right."

Goal-setting gives us confidence that we are doing something with our lives. Developing goals that are closely tied to our dreams and potentials can be a means of actualizing those dreams and potentialities. Goals rooted in our core of self can have the effect of bringing that self out of bondage, freeing dreams that may have long been buried.

Let's find a way to create realistic "birthing goals." The implication that a good or worthwhile woman must do everything at once is unrealistic and unfair. Each woman can realize instead that she has many different phases in her life. Part of her identity can be invested in each phase.

Women today can set goals compatible with their talents and their present lives. There is no need to panic—time will keep opening up new possibilties; something that is not feasible in one phase may be perfect in another. Ten years ago I would not have attempted to write this book; I would not have had the interest, the time, the background, or the courage.

Your achievement goals can reflect the stage of life you are in, and the success you seek. They can reflect a balance of home, family, and "work." You don't have to trade one for the other. There are a host of opportunities, as you creatively approach your Life/Work. God Himself, the Master of creative opportunities, is not hemmed in by your limitations or circumstances. He can even help you overcome insurmountable hurdles. "With your help I can advance against a troop; with my God I can scale a wall."[24] You can ask God to help you with your life's goals and trust Him to help you carry them out, even if there are obstacles to their fulfillment. You probably can't do everything on your own, anyway. I certainly can't.

The next exercise is to take your dreams and break them down into personal goals. These should be focused goals, stating what you want to accomplish. Your goals can be anything from starting a business, building a career, writing a book, starting a volunteer service that helps others, and so on. Study the dream statement you filled out earlier, "Where Do I Want to Go?" to help you determine your personal goals.

What goal or goals does this dream suggest? Try to express your dream in the form of a goal that can further your desires for a Life/Work. Be as specific as you can at this point in your journey.

B. My focused dream goals of what I want to achieve and want to become or to do, according to the dreams I have for my future:
(These goals indicate the direction I want to go.)

_____

_____

_____

_____

Now test your goals. Are they realistic? Do they fulfill

your talents, temperament, priorities? If so, you can feel pleased you have identified goals you find worthwhile.

I once had the experience of observing how the lack of goals and of hope can devastate women. I was attending an inspirational seminar in Florida that stressed goal-setting as a way to direct one's life.

About thirty of us were sitting in a circle as the moderator asked us to go around the circle and, one at a time, tell what our life goal or goals were. When it came each woman's turn to share her goals and thoughts, I was stunned by what happened next. About half of the women in the group were either visibly shaken by the question or were in tears. Almost all were searching for a purposeful activity or meaningful tasks. They would have given anything for a goal, because this would have meant they had a purpose and an objective for their lives. It seemed amazing to me that in this so-called sophisticated age so many women still were struggling with some of life's basic needs, especially the need for creative work. I wondered how many of their husbands knew of their hurt and plight.

At least some of the women did walk away from our meeting challenged to find such a goal. They knew what it felt like to have hopes thwarted and longings unfulfilled and were eager to find something they could believe in. "Hope deferred makes the heart sick, but a longing fulfilled is a tree of life" (Proverbs 13:12).

Now that you have your personal goals, you are ready to ask the third question we posed earlier, "How do I get to where I want to go?" While you have begun to determine direction for your life, you will also need to determine the strategies necessary to help you get "there." Someone once aptly said, "Getting there is half the battle."

Your best strategy will lie in striking that critical balance between your resources and goals. The activity/venture you decide on should fulfill your goals and at the same time draw on your greatest abilities and strengths to achieve those goals.

**Discovering
How To Get There**

The strategies you choose will not be without risk, nor will they always lead you to safe places. By considering strategies and resources together, however, you can find the degree of risk that is acceptable to you. To be a risk-taker is scary, but you will be taking a calculated risk. Here too you can commit your plans to God. We are told we should make plans—counting on God to direct us. It is important for you to believe that God wants to take an active part in directing your life.

Let's hear from one woman who was successful in finding the strategies that worked for her life. Louise achieved what she wanted because she understood her resources, decided what her goals were, and then struck that necessary balance between the two. Louise is a resident of Southern California who created something new and exciting in her life when she used her own imagination and initiative in a most unusual way. Her story began when she "saw" a unique opportunity, and did something about it.

Several years ago while traveling in France, she noticed a line of bright-colored clothing designed by a man named Courreges. She felt that California would be the perfect place for his style, and found that Courreges had never established boutiques in the United States.

Louise became excited about the prospect of introducing the line in America. She had stationery printed up with the name "L.D. Enterprises," and wrote Mr. Courreges a letter. She did this in spite of the fact she had never taken a course in marketing, merchandising, or retailing. She had never before had any firsthand experience in selling clothes or in managing a store. However, Louise loved people, liked clothing, and had a father, an oriental rug merchant, who once told her, "Everything is a selling job!"

Louise's Story

This all started with an idea—because I saw a designer I thought would be good for California and it occurred to me that I could do something with that idea. Before I wrote my letter, I talked to a lawyer who dealt with French people and he helped me to write it. But I tried to make my letter different. I talked about how much I loved the clothes, how much I believed in them, and that I wanted to meet with Mr. Courreges.

I wondered if I were doing the right thing, but a friend said, "Louise, don't talk about it, do it." (She was later to become my first customer.) However, some friends were negative and some merchants wondered what I knew about retailing. I listened but I decided nothing ventured, nothing gained. I was excited!

Four days after sending my letter I received an airmail reply: "We are interested. Come to Paris for talks."

The *Los Angeles Times* called to interview me, and did, and I remember saying, "If you have a goal you can do it. You must believe in it." As a result of that article, two banks in L.A. read it and contacted me to say they would lend me money. I did not have my own capital. It was a joy. I had worked hard, my family was proud, and everyone had helped.

I went to Paris and on the last evening of my stay, Courreges gave me his answer. "I will put my trust in you. I will help you in every way I can."

I very much wanted my venture to succeed but more important I wanted my family unit to remain as it was. I told them I would probably have less time to spend with them and I wanted them to understand why.

Some time later I opened a second and third store and it became big business. It was wonderful. A great experience. Eleven years passed before I began thinking about selling my enterprise. I had a good buyer. It was meant to be.

Before I started my enterprise I would often say, "What am I doing?" But like having a baby, once you have it you are so glad. And things have worked out well.

Women can follow their own intuition, not try to prove anything or to compete with others, but do something for their own satisfaction. They can please themselves. I did. It was creative, I wanted to do it, and I'm glad that I did. If a woman has an idea, she should not be afraid to pursue it.

As you start to outline strategies for your life, remember that the creative strategies best for you:

● are consistent with your own nature, your resources, strengths, and motivations.

● are consistent with your goals.

● strike a balance between your resources and your goals.

● offer the degree of risk you feel comfortable with.

● are given to God.

Record your strategy for directing your Life/Work, telling how you will accomplish it. Does your strategy strike a balance between your resources and goals?

_____

_____

_____

_____

Add this strategy to your growing Life/Work Chart and describe also your risk/reward ratio and the kind of venture that could be right for you.

III. How Can I Get to Where I Want to Go?

A. My best strategy to get to where I want to go, balancing my resources and my goals:

_____

_____

_____

_____

B. My risk/reward ratio (based on taking a calculated risk):

1. What I feel I have to offer or can risk; or, describe how you are minimizing risk.

_____

_____

_____

2. What I feel I have to gain; or, describe why it would be worth taking a risk.

_____

_____

_____

C. What kind of activity could present an acceptable

risk factor? Describe the *type* of opportunity that could best match your risk quotient. For example: My creative activity should be one that balances my resources (a restating of abilities) and my goals (a restating of goals). _____

_____

_____

_____

_____

You are now at a crossroad, a crossover point, the place or juncture where you have to decide upon the activity or enterprise that could use your best talents and further your goals.

Your opportunity may be just around the corner. Keep searching, for given time, what is right will prevail. Don't concern yourself with the outcome as yet, but with the effort you are putting forth. Ask yourself only, "Am I on the right path?" If you can answer that affirmatively, you are well on your way.

Chapter Four

Designing Your Creative Venture

I will instruct you and teach you in the way you
should go; I will counsel you and watch over you.
Psalm 32:8-9

As you think about your goals you may be starting to feel
more than a little excited about them. You are starting to
understand what you're looking for and the venture/
activity that would be most ideal for you. With your excitement, however, you may also feel concern and may wonder, "Can I really make my own dreams come true?" The
reality of bringing your dreams to fruition is enough to
allow a fear to rise within you and hold you back—the fear
of failure. This fear often strikes just as you are about to
take action. A voice whispers in your ear, "It is not too
late. You can quit now. No one will ever know. Besides, it
is a lot safer where you are."

You are not the first, nor will you be the last, to have to
conquer this fear. It seems to be a normal reaction when
one is involved in a new endeavor. We have all no doubt
felt that fear at different times in our lives. Stretching ourselves can be scary, as can be the living out of our dreams.
Part of this stretching is a recognition that we are responsible for our lives; we must be willing to assume the responsibility for our own future. Such recognition is necessary before we can go any further with our hopes and
dreams. We have not really begun our journey toward

meaning until we have wholeheartedly committed ourselves to the goals we have set out to achieve. There comes a time for each of us to put fear behind, and even to leave comfort zones that we've established as safe harbors for our lives.

What can you do as you strike out and look for ways to use your talents more fully? You can start by looking for ideas to build a strong enterprise, formed from your own conception of what you want to be or do. Those ideas can help define the activity and the excellence you desire.

Ideas are the seeds that have started many a successful enterprise, and seed ideas, like the enterprises they start, also start small. There are certain characteristics of the ideas that make for successful entrepreneuring. You can benefit from knowing what they are, regardless of what you are planning to do.

The Entrepreneurial Idea

A good entrepreneurial idea usually represents a better product, a needed service, an improved way to do something, or a new technology. That idea can be in one small but specific area. The fact that the idea has a narrow focus or is concentrated may make it all the more effective. An idea that tries to include too much, that has too broad a scope, may be unwieldy and counterproductive to carry out. An idea for a successful business also would define a "product" with potential to produce profit.

Your idea may be for a better product, a necessary service, or even a better society. It may be small, but it can represent whatever you think would make a meaningful contribution, would satisfy a need, would solve a problem, or would serve a particular segment of society. Developing a small business is the favorite career switch for women in this decade. You may not be changing careers, but you will not be alone if you decide to start a small enterprise. Your idea may have the potential to produce profit, to help others, or to serve social reform, and you can decide whether economic results are to be a part of that service.

No idea is without risk. But you have been evaluating that risk, and your ideas have been rooted in the dreams you feel God has given you. The best strategies of business will never replace constantly submitting your ideas and plans to the One who is the source of creative ideas, and the sower of dreams!

We've talked about what the typical entrepreneurial idea usually suggests: a good product or a needed service. Now let's talk about finding a good idea for *you*. There are two parts that make an idea a good one: first, the idea is based on one's own potential or ability to act upon that idea, and second, the idea has potential, or viability in the marketplace. If your ideas can pass this double test, you can be reasonably sure you have found a good idea for your venture or Life/Work.

Let's first take a look at finding an idea that is based on your potentials. Before you explore any ideas you might have, two young women will tell how they considered ideas for an activity based on their own potential. Laurie's and Misha's stories may help you as you think through and examine your own ideas.

Laurie is a college graduate who has worked in a retail shop/cooking school. She feels this helped prepare her for her future, as well as giving her greater experience and understanding of herself. As Laurie makes plans, she knows she would like to create an entrepreneurial activity around her abilities and interests. She had to go through a careful thought process and a series of steps, before she found the idea that really excited her and could utilize her talents.

Laurie's Story

My problem in college was integrating my interests with something that would support me once I was on my own. I grew up with a fascination with psychology, but an impatient nature; I grew up with a fascination for business, but no desire to study economic theory for four years. After college I channeled these two interests into working in a retail business that had home and kitchen products and a cooking school. That was an education all its own. I gained a knowledge of the workings of a small business, invaluable for starting something of my own, and I learned more about people.

I have other and new ideas, however, that appeal to me. I have gone back to an idea which I developed at the end of college—having to do with an innovative concept in catering.

I've taken, therefore, my real, true and primary joy of cooking and planned how I can funnel it into an activity which can also use my writing, business, and psychology interests and abilities. This activity will offer a unique service to people who desire a caterer, and who desire dining to be more than a meal. My idea and activity will encompass my own needs and best resources to implement it.

It has also taken a year and a hard-nosed mentor to make me realize that no time will ever be better than now, and if I want to pursue my idea at all, I'm the only one who can make it come alive. And should I never try, I may not only regret it, but also may wonder if I could have made my dream as big as I thought it could be.

The potential for success is always equal to the potential for failure. But if I never take even a little chance, I will never give myself that opportunity. My success is measured somewhat in terms of my ability to take risks and survive the results. I am an independent person and meeting someone else's standards in order to become a success does not appeal to me. I have my own standards, my own goals, and my own way of doing things.

My activity will give me the opportunity to see

how far I can take an idea and a dream. It's a chance to prove I can really do something like this, and an opportunity—if it comes off—to make money.

Misha also graduated from college and has a master's degree in education from Harvard. As she thinks about her future, she is wondering what she can do with her talents.

Misha's Story

I've got to be me. The talents and abilities I have, God's given me for a purpose. It's obvious to me I'm not meant to be a banker or a computer technician. God has given me a definite ability with children. I feel I also have common sense, an ability to organize, and a way of seeing with a child's eye.

I also am trained in counseling people. Through the years I've done a lot of different things such as working with disturbed children, supervising in a hospital, counseling at a prep school, all of which I've enjoyed. But they haven't encompassed the full me.

I've often thought of what I could do with what God has given me that would integrate more of what I like and do well. It has taken me some time to figure out a way in which I can enjoy serving God and also use my talents.

When I was obtaining my Masters of Education at Harvard I wrote a long paper on children's literature, and relished doing the research and reading. I've also taught kindergarten and first grade. While doing that I discovered that educational games are such fun nowadays. I've even thought, "Wouldn't it be great if children had more comfortable clothes to wear as they play?"

My desire to work with and be around children has led me to think of several approaches to put some of my ideas to use. One is to be a guidance counselor, but that would restrict other creative juices. My main idea is to open a shop in a location where parents are concerned with their children's personal growth. In the shop I could provide consultant and guidance support, as well as comfortable clothing, educational toys and a select group of inspirational children's literature. There must be books available where kids could learn godly principles in a modern world, and if there aren't I'll write them!

This is not the only thing I want to do with my life, but it is the one way I can focus my talents. I'm sure God will grant me the opportunity to stick my finger in many pies. All I want to do is serve Him the best I can.

With Misha's bubbling enthusiasm, personal abilities, and faith, I am sure she will succeed in whatever she undertakes.

**Designing
My Ideal Life/Work**

The information you have about your own abilities can help you find the ideas that will go into forming a Life/Work activity or project. Your talents, your "heart and hand" experiences that you found satisfying, your uniqueness, dreams, and goals are the many pieces that can provide the ideas and the choices you now have. These creative parts that you've already defined can help design a venture that is perfect for you, and that represents a natural way for you to express yourself. If you have an interest in art, in serving, in teaching, in music, in design, in computers, in cooking, that interest can be turned into a creative activity or business you would find as rewarding as Laurie and Misha. You have many choices to consider.

In the past choices were often limited to either-or. Either women had a career or they stayed home; either they were a teacher or they were a nurse; either they sacrificed themselves totally to serve others, or they served their own needs and sacrificed the needs of others: either they did nothing at all, or they felt they had to "have it all" or "be it all." Today you don't have to be hemmed in by such a narrow perspective, and by such limiting choices.

I have included the visual, My Activity, to show how you can construct an activity that is ideal for you. You can design it to fit your own priorities, potential, and the place where you may be in your life. As other women have done, your activity can be designed around your present roles. It can include your own combination of talents, wants, and needs.

The drawing represents you and your many creative aspects.

As you study this diagram, think about the activity that could tap what motivates you most, could incorporate your abilities and uniqueness, and could further your dream-goals. In chapter 3, you noted the kind of venture that could contain each of these elements; now, describe in fuller detail the exact nature of that project/venture, and what it will be.

See if you can enlarge your vision and stretch your thinking from what you've previously written down. You are building on previously recorded information and on the awareness you've gained.

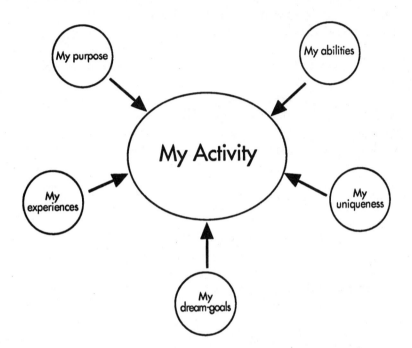

● Begin by writing a list of several ideas, each time describing the activity or enterprise that would be based on your own creative potential.

An Exercise To Design Your Own
Activity or Life/Work:

1. To help get you started, describe the activity or activities that express your own purposes or mission.

_____

_____

_____

_____

_____

2. If you were using your favored abilities, and resources, what would you be doing? For the time being
forget any other considerations. Forget whether your
present circumstances or past achievements coincide with
your new ideas. What activity could capture your best
abilities?

_____

_____

_____

_____

_____

3. What activity or activities do you feel could take advantage of your own uniqueness, which is to say the total
you—what motivates you, the talents you have, and the
way you use them. (Those discoveries are part of your
chart.) What would you do if you could do what is most
ideal to you? Would you be performing a service, starting a
business, creating a product, or would you be engaged in
some kind of creative project? Write a description of the
activity or activities you think are most suited to you, paying attention to the details of these questions.

_____

_____

_____

_____

4. Describe an activity that could fulfill your dreams for
achievement and your personal goals.

_____

_____

_____

_____

Some of what you are writing may seem repetitive; actually, you are expanding on earlier data. After a while, certain things will start to stand out. You will probably discover, as I did, that even though you are describing many activities or ventures that could incorporate who you are, some will definitely interest and motivate you more.

What I found so interesting in doing an exercise like this is that some ideas captured more of me—not only my resources, but my strongest motivations and values. I had thought of doing several things, but always within the framework and setting of business, because that had been my background. But as I saw myself carrying out my interests in other ways; and by changing the setting I imagined being in, I was able to find ideas that really motivated me. Thinking about helping women with their personal struggles and challenges to put their own talents and faith to the test, was much more gratifying than thinking about knocking on business doors and helping women sell ten widgets instead of five. My decision became an easy one, when I looked at my options from a motivational standpoint.

You have written a description of the activities that could draw on your own abilities and resources. Is there one idea/activity that appeals to you? That idea should also give you a feeling of "rightness" about it. Psychologists would call it the "aha" syndrome, when you find an idea that "clicks" and gives you a feeling of security and centeredness. But that security hopefully is also coming from God's leading. It could be your ideas are starting you down a path you would not have taken, because it seems an improbable one as you understand things. Your part is just to trust a wisdom higher than your own. God has promised to "instruct you and teach you in the way you should go," and "counsel you and watch over you."

● Now, combine the answers you've recorded into one descriptive statement. That may call for rewriting and refining, but you should be able to express the idea (and activity) that represents the best one for you.

If you are having trouble stating your idea clearly, you may want to use some sources that could stimulate ideas. *The Occupational Handbook* by the Department of Labor should be at your local library. You can consult the current edition of *What Color is Your Parachute*, by Richard Bolles,[1] or *Finding a Job You Could Love*, by Arthur Miller and Ralph Mattson,[2] and *The Eighth Day of Creation* by Elizabeth O'Connor,[3] books with a spiritual perspective. These books are excellent if you need to further pursue exploring creative ideas for a Life/Work.

Finding Creative Ideas

• Describe the activity that encompasses and balances your strongest motivations, talents, and goals.

_____

_____

_____

_____

Is this activity one that truly motivates and inspires you to pursue it? If this is the case, you will want to add your definition to your Life/Work Chart. Before you do, however, does your idea pass the second test of a good idea, that it has market potential of its own? Let's test your idea and activity against the requirements of business. These requirements can help fine tune any ideas you may have, regardless of the activity you are planning.

Finding Ideas with Potential

How would a business person or an entrepreneur go about deciding if an idea had potential? To meet the standards of business, such ideas would need to define:

-a viable product
-a legitimate "customer" or client
-the market where that customer is
-the benefit to the customer
-a meaningful contribution

If this sounds like a lot, it is. However, a breakdown in any one of these areas can result in the breakdown of an idea, or worse, of the success of a venture. An enterprise that can't clearly define itself is an enterprise that is risking failure. You can examine your own ideas with the same criteria in mind. These standards can help you determine whether your ideas have merit.

As you look at ideas that could have potential for your Life/Work activity, keep in mind that a product is *whatever* you may be offering others, and a customer is *whoever* is buying or using that product. It need not be a product and customer as commonly thought of. In nonprofit activities, the product is the service you are offering, and the customer is the person who gains something from that service.

● A Good Idea Defines the Product. The first requirement for an idea is that it defines what is being offered, the "product" or service the idea has conceived. What do we mean by a product? Theodore Leavitt, Professor of Business Administration at Harvard University and author, has said that a product is the "synthesis of what the seller intends and the buyer perceives."[4] It is the total cluster of value satisfactions being offered, satisfactions that differentiate it from other products or offerings. A product, in sum, is a combination of both what the "seller" is offering and what the "buyer" is hoping he will receive.

Has the idea you have written for your creative activity defined the product or service your idea has conceived? You may need to enlarge on your ideas for that product or service. Don't think just in terms of what you are presenting, but in terms of what the person using it would be looking for. What would he or she want from it? It may surprise you to think from someone else's perspective. Your product or service is the entire package of satisfactions you are providing, and therefore your description should include all of them. What you plan to offer and what others want, may be two different things.

For instance, your "product" might be offering a service of total home care—i.e., house cleaning, light repair work, even buying groceries, and baby-sitting, and "customers" may only want to pay for part of those services. Your product should represent what others desire from it, not what you insist they should have.

If your product satisfactions fill the needs of others, you have a valid idea for a product, whatever that product is.

My Product or Service

_____

_____

_____

_____

● A Good Idea Defines the Customer or Market. The customer is the person a business would direct its product to, or whoever stands to benefit the most from it. This could encompass a wide range including those who will need it more, or it could be a narrow range, but a very specific group of people. The nature of the product itself will usually define who its users are. If that range is quite small or has a limited customer potential, the customer should be able to get something from that product he or she may have a hard time getting somewhere else, or getting in that fashion.

A business would then make a list of any and all possible customers for a product, and rate them in order of the best customers to the more marginal ones. This would insure that the product would be used where it could fill a genuine need and could bring the greatest return.

If the customer base is deemed not big enough, a business would reexamine its idea to see what redefining was needed, or whether the idea should be discarded. Without a customer base, an idea or product is not viable.

Has your idea and product defined who could benefit from that product or service? Ask yourself, "Who would most use my service or product? Are there enough people who need or value what I am doing? *Make a list of all potential groups of "customers."* For example: you may be providing a service of taking shut-ins or elderly people for drives or errands, and you may charge for your service or you may not, depending on if you are doing this for volunteer reasons or for profit. You still need to define the people you would be helping, and need to make a list of preferred "customers" to determine if you have enough of a customer base for your venture.

Separate your customers into categories of those you think would use or want it and those who might be on the fringe.

The Customer My Idea Defines

My Target Customers

1. _____

2. _____

3. _____

My Possible Customers

1. _____

2. _____

3. _____

Ask, "Does my customer base cover a wide range, or does it focus on a very small but specific group of people?" If you're not sure, or if your idea doesn't offer value to others, you may need to reexamine it. If you have a limited customer potential, your ideas should focus exactly on the unique aspects of your product and on who it is for.

• A Good Idea Defines the Market or Niche. A market is where the preferred customer is, or where he or she can be found. This also suggests different ways or channels that can be used to reach him or her. Growth for an enterprise comes from offering a certain market what it wants, and from knowing *where* that market is. Later on the market can be enlarged, as there is opportunity to expand the products or services that fall within it.

Is there a "market" your customer has defined? Where does the person or opportunity exist for what you are offering? The "who" really answers the "where." Look at the statement of who your customer is. Where does that person reside—where is his world? If you don't know, you should. Your market can be anywhere the person or customer you hope to reach can be found!

From the description you wrote listing your target customers, write a description of the places you think that "customer" would be. Try to define your "market."

For example: We mentioned a service activity of helping the elderly or shut-ins. If you were to start this activity you would want to figure out where these people live. This would involve talking to or visiting nurse associations, talking to nursing homes, and to retirement community staff leaders who would know who in their community is housebound, or limited in their ability to get out on their own. Once you identify where your market is, in this case shut-ins, it is so much easier to figure out *how* to reach that market. Again, using our example above, you could send brochures or letters to be posted on bulletin boards in nursing homes, you could send letters to shut-ins in retirement communities, and you could send letters or a brochure describing your service to people that a visiting nurse might suggest.

Ask yourself if you really understand your market, and what you have to do to reach it.

The Market My Idea/Product Has Defined and How To Reach It

_____

_____

_____

_____

After the ideas of a business defined the market it is serving, the business would better know what that market is looking for.

● A Good Idea Defines the Benefits or Value Satisfactions. Just as every product defines a market, there are value satisfactions each market seeks from that product.

A business would try to define what its own market wants, and how its products or services can help to meet those needs.

What are the satisfactions your proposed "product" or creative activity will deliver? What are you providing your "customer" and your "market," that can help fill their wants and needs or help solve their problems? Understanding your customer should have given you an understanding of what he/she might be looking for from you. Put yourself in his or her shoes and ask what you would want from your own service or product if you were using it yourself!

Define the satisfactions you are delivering. For instance, again using our example: elderly and shut-ins would value the ability to go outdoors, to expand their world, to do necessary errands, to have companionship and to feel more a part of everyday life. What are the value satisfactions your product offers? You may also be giving people love and caring concern for their well-being. That is an added dimension you can offer with your service.

The Satisfactions My Product Offers

_____

_____

_____

_____

The final thing the ideas of business would try to define is the contribution it hopes to make. The entrepreneurial contribution has usually been to bring innovation or change to society or to the world, and therefore a business would make every attempt to define its own contribution as well as its products or services.

A business would sum things up by asking, "Are we making a worthwhile contribution?" That offering has usually been one of providing something benefiting other people. However, bottom line interests that a product or service be sold profitably also are a driving force. If the business has done a good job of giving people a product or service that can help them and can solve some problem, economic results will follow. That is the ideal, but not all products offer a meaningful contribution. Yours can, as you commit yourself to integrity and excellence that goes beyond the norm.

What can your venture and idea offer, or what is the contribution you want to make? Your best creative effort will be work that helps others and honors God. I know a woman who volunteered the use of her home to parents visiting critically ill children at a Boston hospital. She provided not only a room, but hospitality and inspirational comfort to those who were suffering. Her contribution was offered free of charge. Yours can also provide a meaningful service and you might ask, "What is *my* bottom-line interest?" Is it to have a product that can be sold profitably and can result in economic performance? Is it to help someone else with personal needs? Or is it to bring about some social reform?

Defining My Contribution

You are free to make whatever contribution you want, in keeping with the activity you are designing. Your contribution may be a product that helps people or markets, but nothing says that contribution has to be measured in terms of dollars and cents. Economic results may follow after "a job well done," but money doesn't have to be the driving force, nor does it have to be a force at all, if you don't want it to be.

You could be helping the elderly, to fill your own needs of serving (maybe you had invalid parents), or you could be doing it to make the world a better place for those less fortunate or unable to help themselves. If you had inspirational objectives, you could even be doing it to advance the kingdom of God on earth. Your contribution can be an act of worshiping God, returning to Him the work of your heart and hands.

The Contribution My Activity Will Make

What is the excellence that will mark that contribution?

How has your idea stood up to the testing? Can it survive on its own merit? Have your ideas measured up to the standards of good entrepreneurial principles, whether you plan on starting a business or not?

Step by step you've finished outlining and designing the activity/venture you think is perfect for you, based on your own potential and based on the potential for a business enterprise! Your activity grew as you filled in your answers to the exercises that were presented in this chapter.

If your venture has met the requirements for a good idea, your activity or work project is one of promise. It should represent what you want to do with your talents and your time, and what you can offer to others. That idea can also represent God's ideas for you, and how He sees you putting your abilities to use.

Write a summary definition of your activity, this time including its product, customer, market and contribution, expanding on your earlier definition of your "ideal" activity. Express in full the product or service you will offer, the customer you will serve, the market you'll concentrate on, and the contribution you'll make.

_____

_____

_____

_____

_____

_____

Could you enjoy doing this activity because it's a place you feel at home? Does it seem the best pathway for your life, the path that is "the way you should go"? Again, if God has been instructing and counseling you in that way, you will have a real peace about it, even if logically it doesn't make sense. If you feel right about your decision, add the definition of your activity to your Life/Work Chart. Before you do, however, ask yourself the same questions a business would ask:

● "Are my ideas capable of providing something that can meet my own needs, as well as the needs of others?"

● "Do my ideas hold the promise of the future I want?"

● "Do I believe in my ideas?"

● "Am I capable of carrying them out?'

● "Do they represent God's plans for me as best I can understand?"

If you can answer these questions affirmatively, transfer the description of your activity to your ongoing chart.

Defining My Creative Activity or Life/Work

_____

_____

_____

_____

_____

You have completed your description of the activity that can bring fuller use of your talents and can help others, and the Life/Work Chart of what you want to do with your life. Now you'll have to take your ideas and turn them into the enterprise or the opportunity you've just outlined and "designed," while going through this chapter.

Turning Your Ideas into Opportunity
Is the opportunity you defined one that will bring your ideas of what you want to be and do into being? That opportunity should be able to carry out your goals, and take advantage of what you do well.

Your opportunity should have a "fit" with you, and match your own experiences, successes and achievements. If that "fit" is a good one, you can assume any risks you might be taking and go ahead with your plans.

Webster defines opportunity as: "a combination of circumstances, favorable for the purpose, and a good chance."[5] Assuming you have seen your opportunity is to assume you have seen the relatedness of your own circumstances—the time is right, the opportunity is right, and you are at the right place in your life where you don't want to miss the chance to do what you would really like to do. Conditions may not be ideal, (are they ever?) but you have an opportunity to put circumstances together creatively to achieve your deepest desires and goals for your life. That awareness could almost be construed as your own invitation from destiny.

Let's talk with two more women who have taken the next part of the journey you are about to embark on. These women of different interests and backgrounds turned their own ideas into a creative activity. In doing so they also created a Life/Work opportunity and circumstances they found to be more favorable.

Let's listen as Jean describes the unique idea at the core of her creative activity/opportunity. Jean sells a line of high-fashion, handcrafted silver jewelry, designed by outstanding artists.

Jean's Story

I would have to say that the core idea of my creative activity has to do with two things; first jewelry and carvings that truly are 'art' and have been made by skilled craftsmen who bring their own knowledge, culture, and tradition to their craft, and two, my own skill in picking art objects that I feel are qualified as being beautiful, well done, and worthy of purchase.

I represent several artists, some of them Native Americans, some Spanish, and some Anglo. They are primarily located in the Southwestern part of the United States. From them I bring back jewelry and wood carvings that are individually designed and hand crafted, and I make them available for sale in the East. These pieces are usually shown in art galleries or at trunk shows. All my items have been personally selected by me, and I often go to the artists' homes to choose from a wide variety of offerings.

What is unique is not just the item itself. There are others who offer similar things. I feel what brings uniqueness to what I am doing is that I choose a body of work carefully that represents my taste, background, circumstances and exposure. All these come into play. Many times there are pieces from a collection that I will not choose and I would not want to offer to others. I have had a lot of contact with the arts, especially because of my husband's interest in art collecting, and this has refined my aesthetic appreciation and knowledge.

I believe also there is a principle that operates for each of us as we act upon our own ideas and carry them out. We each bring to what we are doing our own uniqueness of talent God has given us, and the circumstances and environment He has placed us in. These all interplay in who we are and in everything we do, and they make a difference. Therefore, we need to be aware of this principle and see how it is operative in our lives and in others.

I strongly feel it is necessary to include both what is unique about my venture and what I uniquely contribute to it, to form that venture. They go hand in hand. I would add that I love what I am doing because I am able to make the statement I just made. I also enjoy bringing a major in psychology, a minor in sociology, interest in biblical principles and in human nature, and lastly a desire to interact with people from other cultures to my efforts. These each are an inherent part of the Life/Work I have chosen.

Let's also hear from Sylvia, and see how she looked at herself and her circumstances, and took advantage of circumstances which were not the best at the time. She formed an activity that was in keeping with her own goals and talents, and found the courage to act on that opportunity.

Sylvia's Story

I was divorced at twenty-nine, with three small daughters to raise alone, no alimony and only a minimum amount of child support. During the sixties, it wasn't easy. I felt driven toward "being a success" in order to make enough money to raise my kids. I had to move to an urban area where there was more opportunity, and work like a maniac. In those days a woman had to be better than all the men around her in order to get ahead.

In my work, there were some exciting years as I strove to get ahead. I created a niche for myself within a prestigious, internationally acclaimed company. Finally I made my way into a category called 'professional staff' which indicated I was to be taken more seriously. Though I didn't have a prestigious title, I had a fair amount of power for someone not officially in a management position.

Eventually I moved back to the semi-rural state I had come from to be close to my family. Though being closer to them gave me comfort, the area I moved into was a low-wage, high-unemployment area. I finally got work—at a twenty-five percent cut in pay.

But, the worst was yet to come. I lost my job, and shortly after my home burned, destroying everything I owned. I escaped miraculously, in my bare feet and nightgown. But everything was gone. I was now fifty, with no money, no job, no roof over my head, no shirt on my back. I became seriously depressed. Somehow (I still don't know where the strength came from) I pulled myself together and got a job as a copy editor on a small magazine about personal computers. This was in 1979, at the beginning of the "computer revolution." I was fascinated. I wanted to buy my own machine, but didn't have enough money to afford it.

Fate wasn't finished with me, however. Not quite a year after the fire, I had an accident in which I sustained a serious injury. For nearly a year I couldn't work at all.

There was something to be gained, however, from my illness. It made me SLOW DOWN AND REST, which I desperately needed to do, but had been so consumed with the drive to survive I had believed it impossible. Now it didn't matter much that I couldn't pay my bills, because the only thing I could do was to rest and try to mend. It gave me time to think. I was off the treadmill, forced off by the most dire circumstances, to be sure; but no longer running at top speed like a lemming desperate to reach the edge of the seacliff.

After about a year, an insurance settlement arising from the accident gave me a little bit of money to experiment with.

I took the time to evaluate. (1) I was so disappointed with trying to work for other people that I knew if there was any way in the world for me to work for myself, that was the thing I wanted most. (2) Despite the battering life had given me, I hadn't totally lost faith in myself. I knew I could deal with people and with adversity. I was a good organizer. I had a superior command of the English language, a flair for writing, a knowledge of computers that was uncommon, top speed on a keyboard, and a broad and varied business background.

So I bought my own personal computer and a high quality printer, turning these machines into a word processing system. I found work first as a word processor with editing skill (the two work nicely together), then as writer/editor, as operator and teacher, and more recently have gotten into typesetting with desktop publishing software. Today, in my late fifties, I have built up an independent activity and a mix of steady customers and assignments and smaller jobs in between which sustains me. I work partly at home and partly at others' facilities. I can set my own pace and work independently. If one piece of work becomes something I don't want to keep up with any longer, I can drop it or replace it with something else. I have my own business identity and have slowly built up a good reputation. It is the most wonderful way to work I have ever experienced. And I will probably keep at it in much the same way, since I enjoy what I am doing.

Sylvia's story reveals some of the emotional and practical challenges faced as she looked for an activity and opportunity worth committing to. She has been rewarded for her efforts.

In the following chapter you will be shown how to actually start the activity you have shaped around your own design of talents. Practical suggestions will be given to help get your ideas off the ground, and to turn your dreams into reality. You can continue to pick and choose the information that is presented, and use it as it applies to your own enterprise. Some of this information while businesslike in nature, continues to have direct application to nonprofit activities.

From your creative ideas you have seen a way you can render a service or meet a need. I hope that your dreams will be fulfilled and your efforts will be fruitful, as you act upon that opportunity!

Part Two

Chapter Five

Writing a Start-Up Plan

May He give you the desire of your heart and make all
your plans succeed.

Psalm 20:4

Your ideas for a creative work that can use your talents
and can provide something of meaning for others, have
continued to grow and to come into focus. You have structured the activity that interests you most, and have filled
out a Life/Work Chart. Can you bring that activity, the
"something out of nothing" heart's desire we spoke of,
into being and make your dreams for your future come
true? This is "roll up your sleeves and get down to work"
time, but also a necessary part of your journey. Depending
on what you've decided you want to do, there are practical
steps to be taken and plans to be carried out as you anticipate starting the enterprise of your choice.

Any start-up activity, regardless of what it is, needs to be
organized at the very beginning. The information you've
recorded in previous chapters on your Chart can be recast
to form a plan written according to the essentials of good
entrepreneurial planning. You will find half of your work,
therefore, is already done.

Plans are valuable for any venture, whether it be a volunteer effort, an entrepreneurial project, or a business. You
will soon realize the benefits of future planning. A strategy
and plan provide you with direction and a constant refer-

ence point. Furthermore, you can use your plan not only as an *operating tool*, but as a *financing tool*, should you need to raise monies or seek additional economic assistance. A written plan gives instant information to a lawyer, accountant or anyone else whose help you may need to enlist, and is of inestimable value.

Before we begin, Joanne shares with us some of her thoughts and the steps she took as she organized her early efforts and venture. Her suggestions are both practical and encouraging, and her story should help you as you launch your own venture or Life/Work project.

Joanne's Story

I was at a point in my life that many women reach when the children begin leaving the nest, and was thinking about the next phase of my life. Having raised five children and having worked since I was sixteen, the last thing I wanted to do was to work. However, my brother moved into the area and took over as director of a skating club. He asked me if I would like to start a boutique at the skating rink. Totally forgetting I didn't want to work, I thought, "Why not?" The two things I know best are figure skating and retailing, my background having been in competitive figure skating and seven years in the Ice Follies, prior to my marriage. My husband and I had started a ski shop and built it successfully into many ski shops in several states. It never dawned on me that I couldn't make this new venture a success.

The difficulty was I had been out of the skating world for many years. I needed to find out what the current trends in skating were. I made my decision overnight, and immediately began asking questions. I'd sit with mothers at the skating rink to find out where they got all the apparel their children were wearing, and how to reach the manufacturer, and I would go home and call the cities the manufacturers were from and would explain what I was doing. Everyone was very generous in giving me more leads, and in sending me to others, as long as they weren't competitors. I'd spend a day at the rink, and a day on the phone. Most of the people sent me samples because they wanted my business. I would take the samples to the rink and get the skaters' opinions as to whether they liked them or not. All my antennae were out. If anyone mentioned a product, I'd ask them where I could get what I needed. From samples, I would call back and ask manufacturers to send me what they thought I could sell, in a size range. This took five months. I also called fifteen contractors to build the shop, before I found one that could have it open and ready for September 20th!

In September there was a skating competition that brought people from all over the Eastern seaboard. At the same time I was ordering stationery, business cards, sales slips, a cash register and so on. Needless to say, I told everyone I had to open September 19th, and there was no difference between day and night leading up to that day. There was difficulty getting things done on time. I was picking out carpeting, paint colors, window treatment, and needed to choose a banker. When I went to the bank I thought all I had to do was tell them I wanted to carry Master Charge and Visa, and they said, "See us in six months." However, I stressed how critical that approval was to my venture, that I had to have it, and gave them all the references I could. Fortunately, they did give me the go-ahead.

To finance my new enterprise I used my savings. I wanted it to be right. (Again, it didn't occur to me that it could fail.) I checked prices, and was very conscious of getting the most from my money in every area. I wanted the store to be a place where people would like to come. Probably the greatest strength I had while preparing for this was I had someone to bounce things off, and that was my brother. He cared about my success as much as I did. It is very hard to do anything alone. You need someone to share things with, or someone who cares.

Whatever the challenge, however, before I would say yes to it, I would do as much foot work as I had time to do. I think everyone sees themselves as an entrepreneur, but few of us have the intelligence to do it all. There is a tendency for us not to use our own gifts and talents from God, and to look at what others are doing and think we should do that too. Starting up an activity is hard enough, so for other women I would say, go into the field you know best, and do what you know best, not what is most romantic or what others are doing well. But, you can do anything you want to do, if you do what's right for you.

Joanne's story evidences the "can do" attitude she has about anything she has put her hand to in her life. Whatever the situation, she has always looked at things positively and had faith in the outcome. This has been of immense help to her through the years. I also know Joanne as someone with a personal faith in God and in God's plans for her, and this has been a guiding force behind all she has ever done or accomplished.

Can you write a plan for yourself and get off to as successful a start as Joanne did? There are several parts that go into making up a good working plan, or business plan, and they should all be included. They are:

- A statement of purpose.
- A description of your product or service, with its uniqueness and appeal to others.
- A detailed section directed at marketing, research, evaluation and strategy.
- A description of competitors, their strengths and weaknesses.

● A financial section that includes a forecast of income and expenses, start-up costs, sales volume by month, a forecast balance sheet, and a cash flow statement.

● A summary of what you bring to an enterprise in resources, experiences, or achievements.

The purpose of this plan is to help you maximize results, opportunities, and resources. Even more, such a plan will enable you to further test your concept and ideas, to see if what you are envisioning will really work.

As your plans are being formed, you can entrust them to God and ask Him to help you with the fulfilling of your heart desires. "May He give you the desire of your heart and make all your plans succeed" (Psalm 20:4). You won't read it in a business book, but God is in the "success" business. And yet another reminder from Proverbs: "To man belong the plans of the heart. . . . Commit to the Lord whatever you do, and your plans will succeed (16:1, 3). God can give a green light to your plans, as your work is given over to Him, but He will determine the outcome.

With that thought in mind, let's begin to establish a good plan for you. As we go through each part, you can tailor it to your own activity or circumstances. If you need a thorough business plan, you can follow item by item; if you don't, you can include only what is needed. Your Life/Work Chart can help in outlining the plan that's best for you. Much of what you will be writing down continues to further focus and enlarge on information you gathered earlier. However, you may need to do some extra research as you write a working plan, and record your findings accordingly.

A Business or Working Plan for My Venture

1. A Statement of Purpose. As you look at your own mission statement and the definition of your "ideal" enterprise on your Chart, the purpose of your activity should also become evident.

Look at your venture's key ideas. Can you write a simple and concise statement of what your enterprise is attempting to do? In writing this statement you could easily miss the essence or define its purpose too narrowly. For example, years ago if the movie industry had defined its mission as being in the "entertainment business" rather than in the movie business, that industry would not have been so alarmed when other forms of entertainment began to appear on the scene. It would have taken the lead in developing other ways of "entertaining" as a part of, and an extension of, its own original purposes.

A definition of purpose should always state the basic nature of what is being done. Another example: A business that manufactures window shades might define itself as being in the "light control business" rather than the "shade business." This would help the company see a host of current and future opportunities. It's a broad enough definition to allow for growth, but narrow enough to force an area of concentration. Or consider the case of IBM. While IBM makes computers and office machines, that is not their purpose or business, but rather offering "word processing and data processing capabilities."

Defining My Purpose

As you examine your ideas, see if you can identify the broader purpose that is at the heart of your venture. Think in terms of the overall objectives you are trying to accomplish. Such purposes should capture the essence of your activity and state the "bigger picture" of what it is all about. For instance, if you were forming a day-care center, you would define your enterprise's purpose as "providing full care for children of working and nonworking parents." This could help you understand that you not only serve people who have daily jobs, but the housewife who may only want to go out for a couple of hours as well. Your mission could later be extended and could include numerous services. And from our earlier example in chapter 4, of a service activity for shut-ins, your stated purpose or intention could be: "providing mobility and care for nonmobile people." This would open up several possibilities as to who could be served and how, again broadening the purpose of an enterprise. Write down the purpose or mission that best expresses the nature of your activity. That venture's purposes should be consistent with, and a furthering of, your own purposes and mission.

The Purpose of My Activity

_____

_____

_____

_____

_____

This purpose should be broadly enough stated to allow for future opportunities, but narrow enough to force a concentrated effort. If you care to, you can add this statement to your Life/Work Chart as IV B. It can be reinforced later in many different ways. It can guide you in product development, in marketing, in advertising, and in all forms of communication. And it can assist in expanding the efforts of a profit or a nonprofit activity, as opportunities present themselves in both. Social purposes can be extended as a venture grows, just as "business" purposes would be. A volunteer service activity whose purpose was to "assist the homeless," could evolve from serving meals to helping the homeless learn crafts and hobbies, using skills that you have. Many shelters today are adding arts and crafts and finding this dimension very helpful, a form of therapy.

2. A Description of Services or Products. This description too is already on your Life/Work Chart and can be incorporated here. You can transfer your "product" description with its features and potentials to your plan. Before doing that, does the description of your product or service need any enlarging upon? Remember, your product is not so much the specific product you are offering, but the *entire cluster of satisfactions* that surround that product, both what you are offering and what others want from it. Curiously, people buy value satisfactions or the expectations of benefits rather than the actual product itself. The definition of your product should help you and others understand the "total product" you are offering, both the tangible and the intangible features.

Before you write a description of your product in your plan, review the features that make up your entire product or service offering. Others may be looking for fast service, low prices, better quality, and so on, and you may be giving them something they don't need or value. You should know what represents the greatest value you can give your potential "customer" or client. This can be incorporated in the description of your "product," whether you are providing a product to be sold, or a volunteer service to be rendered. For example, if you were selling imported clothing, your product definition could be a "high fashion line of imported clothing with a European styling and look." If you were offering a service of home care and cleaning, it could be "providing all the maintenance and care needs of your home," (suggesting everything from cleaning, to small repairs, to home-sitting or vacation-checking by trained home maintenance professionals). If you were volunteering to help disadvantaged people or to provide assistance with civic and social concerns, your "product" description could be: "providing a service assisting in all areas of social and physical need" (suggesting diversity of helping the homeless, visiting the sick or shut-ins, even calling on widows and orphans). This product description while offering services, also incorporates almost a biblical injunction of caring for others. It states what is being offered (services) and to whom, (those who require help either practically or personally).

Restate the product or service you are offering, including what others want from it. It is taken from your chart and broadened to include the tangible and intangible features.

My Product Description or Definition

_____

_____

_____

_____

_____

3. The Market, Marketing Plans, and Market Strategies. This can include your "customer" and market size, trends and segments. It can detail your overall marketing strategy, sales tactics, and any advertising and promotion you may plan to do for your product or service. Much of this information also is on your Chart, and can be restated to cover these issues and added to your plan.

Look at the previous definition of your customer and market. Have you fully described your major "customer" group and your secondary customer group? You need to describe both, and the market in which they can be found, in your business plan. You have noted your best "customer" in order of preference or priority and have stated "where" that person is. However, your ideas may have continued to grow. If so, include any additional insights you may have gained. Be sure to list all sources of information that may have been used to make these projections.

Give a general idea of the size of your market, paying attention to special segments or trends within it. It can be a challenge to determine who your "real" customer is. You need to be aware of the people who would most benefit from your help. They are your "customers," if you will. In nonprofit activities, children, homeless people, the elderly, unwed mothers or teenagers may be your "clients." To make sure your customer base is covered, ask a few more questions:

Is there anyone else who could benefit from my services or product? List that person or persons.

_____

_____

_____

_____

Where are they? Name those places.

_____

_____

_____

Where should my service, therefore, be made available?

_____

_____

_____

Are you getting an idea of the size of your market and where it exists?

Go on to explain how you plan to enter your market. Whatever is of most importance or most critical to you, present those facts in detail. For instance, if advertising and promotion are critical to your enterprise, you would tell how you would plan to advertise and promote. The character of your activity will always determine the strategies you use, or whether any strategies are needed. For example: selling clothing or jewelry, either at home parties or by private invitation parties, would require strategies to contact women who would hold these events. Some promotion would be important for the success of your efforts. Those strategies would have to be identified. Another example: if you were serving a "market" for social purposes and needs, i.e., the homeless, nursing homes, troubled teenagers, etc., your strategies could include writing a brochure describing your services, calling on heads of social agencies, and finding out where needs are the greatest.

List your strategies to reach your market in order of preference:

_____

_____

_____

_____

_____

Finally the marketing section of your plan should explain in more detail the *estimated market share* and *market growth forecast*. Also it should fully describe any *special advertising or promotion* you plan to do and any *special policies, selling* or *distribution* that are needed.

When you have an understanding of the marketing area, include your findings above, as well as information recorded before about your product, in step 3 of your business plan.

My Marketing Plans, Evaluation of
Market Share and Market Strategy

Marketing:_____

_____

_____

Evaluation of Market Share:_____

_____

_____

Market Strategy:_____

_____

_____

4. Competition. As you detail your marketing efforts, start to think about step four of your business plan, *competition*. If you're thinking of a traditional business, you should know who your key competitors are, along with their strengths and weaknesses, and estimated market share. In a volunteer activity you should be aware of who may be doing something similar, and whether it is being performed in a different way than yours will be. This can suggest how you might carry out your own service activity, or suggest extra features you may want to add to your service.

Who are your competitors? If you're not sure, look in the yellow pages, talk to the Chamber of Commerce, the Small Business Association, or to anyone who is in your industry or in your area of interest. You may want to do some additional research. *Make a list of competitors and what they offer.* Get to know more about them and know also what is unusual about what you are doing.

_____

_____

_____

What about your enterprise? Are you planning to be a leader and an innovator, or a follower and an imitator? If you have a "product," a good rule of thumb is that it should have at least three advantages over any competition in order to justify its existence. These could be in quality, performance, cost, service, appearance, faster delivery and so on. If you have a nonprofit service activity, you can also describe the advantages of what you are doing, in comparison to others. For instance: If you are volunteering to visit ailing or older people in hospitals and nursing homes, what added services could you offer other than just "visiting"? Name three advantages of your product or service:

_____

_____

_____

_____

With new services, there often are limitations that new products may not have. Competition is keener because service is an easier area to enter, with less capital needed to start. Advantages over competitors have to be obvious in a service industry. List your competitors, and state how your product or service differs from theirs.

My Competition

_____

_____

_____

_____

_____

5. Financial Considerations. This section applies particularly to a business enterprise. However, a nonprofit enterprise should manage itself as responsibly as a profit-mak-

ing enterprise, and be held equally accountable. The financial section of your plan should contain a forecast of income and expenses, and a balance sheet. A cashflow analysis, break-even charts, and a profit and loss forecast should also be included.

Most entrepreneurial ventures are financed by the owners until a collateralized lending stage has been reached. Gradually the venture is supported by the assets and funds generated by the business itself. Collateral lending usually begins sometime during the third and fourth years. However, you may require economic assistance in the beginning, rather than later. Either way it is good to plan and to document your financial needs and projections accordingly. For the purpose of our discussion here, let's talk in terms of starting a business.

In considering financial requirements, a business would normally require two kinds of operating funds. The first would be working capital or cash, money to be used for buying and replenishing inventory, paying salaries and the day-to-day expenses such as utilities, rent, taxes, and insurance. The second would be capital expenditures which would be for equipment that is needed, or for improvements in working facilities. These monies would also pay for any startup costs involved in advertising, telephone or electrical installation, etc.

The plan for your requirements is called a feasibility study. Forecasts of income and expenses would be part of this study and would be done every month in the beginning years. (Any potential lender would look at these projections very carefully.) An accountant can help you put your projections together. Here are some guidelines for what those projections should show, and for what to record in your business plan.

My Financial Plan

A. Estimated Expenses Per Month—(cover all costs) Include telephone, insurance, utilities, salaries, rent, office supplies and equipment, advertising and postage, inventory, consultation fees and promotion. Be generous with any estimates because this will add up to more than you think.

My costs per month are: (list the above items separately)
1. Telephone_____
2. Insurance_____
3. Utilities_____
4. Salaries_____
5. Rent_____
6. Office supplies_____
7. Advertising and postage_____
8. Inventory_____
9. Consultation fees_____
10. Promotion_____

B. Start-up Costs. Include telephone installation, equipment purchases, inventory needs, decoration and fixtures, salaries, taxes, and printing costs for stationery and brochures. Include how much capital will be needed to operate your venture in the beginning.

My start-up costs are: (list similar to the expenses per month above)
1. Telephone installation_____
2. Equipment purchases_____
3. Inventory needs_____
4. Decoration and fixtures_____
5. Salaries_____
6. Taxes_____
7. Printing costs, stationery/brochures_____
8. Capital needed to operate_____

C. Expected Sales Volume by Month. In addition to start-up costs, financial projections for a minimum of two or three years can be included. (We'll discuss a pro forma statement and balance sheet soon.) When your projections are ready, add at least ten percent as a protection against inflation and use this figure as the amount of money you will need. Actually, after determining the essential amount of capital, a capital investment that provides a twenty to forty percent extra cushion is even better. That "cushion" hedges against undercapitalization and compensates for any mistakes or setbacks that may occur. Lack of sufficient economic resources, or underestimating monies needed, is a common cause of the premature failure of an enterprise.

Sales projections can be itemized as realistically as possible for each category of products or items. In a service business the number of clients or customers would be forecast, and you would take the expected number of monthly clients or services and multiply by your estimated dollar average per client.

Record your expected sales volume by the month and capital needs:

My Expected Sales Volume by Month

_____

_____

_____

_____

Not having strong financial planning can be the undoing of an otherwise strong business. By the time a business realizes it needs more capital, it may not have the time or ability to react soon enough to prevent the collapse of the business.

How good a job you do at figuring your financial needs will be a key factor in presenting an economic proposal to anyone.

Business planners in stationery stores can help you organize your finances. Retired executives who belong to a nationwide organization called SCORE, can provide planning and "hands-on" consultation at no cost.

Cash flow statements, which record the rate of money coming in and out of a business, as well as where it is going, can be done to project three different growth potentials—low, average, and better than average. You will have to decide which you think applies to you. Add a cash flow statement also to your plan.

D. A Cash Flow Statement. Estimate the amount of cash that you anticipate will be flowing in and out of your venture. You'll have to do a cash flow analysis, either monthly or quarterly.

A cash flow statement should cover two areas:
- Sources of cash—

Whatever brings money in, such as sale of services or products, capital from loans, or money earned on interest.
- Cash going out—

What must be spent to keep your venture operating, such as supplies, overhead, inventory, payment of loans.

My Cash Flow Statement

1. Cash Coming In:
sale of services or products: _____
money earned in interest: _____
capital on loans: _____

_____

2. Cash Going Out: _____
supplies: _____
overhead: _____
inventory: _____
payment of loans _____

_____

(You can later compare each month to show if you are generating more or less cash than before.)

Understanding how much cash you have to spend can

help in other areas of decision. Cash flow can be balanced and compensated for in slower times. Cash flow projections can also help show the amount of capitalization you will need as you go along.

You can include a pro forma statement, which is a forecast for a new business, and takes a look at the future. This is an estimate and is usually for one year. Well documented and mixed with your own enthusiastic presentation, however, this statement could inspire excitement from any potential investor.

An *accountant* can assist with your pro forma statement and pro forma balance sheet. This statement is a summary of the records of your business and contains an income statement of how much you made or lost during a period of time, along with a balance sheet. The balance sheet lists the assets of your activity and the claims on those assets. Assets can be current assets, fixed assets, or long term items, and intangible assets that have no physical nature, such as your trade name or a patent. A balance sheet summarizes the financial position of an enterprise at any given time. You can prepare an early balance sheet which can be enlarged on as your activity grows. Record your pro forma statement and balance sheet in your business plan.

E. My Pro Forma Statement and Pro Forma Balance Sheet. My forecast: (A summary of how much is expected to be made or lost during the first year.) _____

_____

_____

_____

_____

_____

_____

_____

My balance sheet: (Listing current, fixed, and long term assets, and claims of those assets.)_____

_____

_____

_____

_____

_____

_____

Your break-even point will be the point at which you start to show a profit. In order to see a realistic picture of your venture-activity, you would tally up the gross profit or all money that comes in, and subtract all your overhead costs and expenses. What is left will be your net, or actual profit.

This finishes your business plan. Your financial analysis, along with your market plans, represent the two most important sections. I would like to add that just as you used your Life/Work Chart to assist you in writing a plan, you can likewise use the information about yourself on that chart to add a sixth point or section to your plan, *the contribution you bring to your enterprise.*

6. The Resources I Bring to My Enterprise. This section can contain the motivation, resources, abilities, experiences and achievements, and personal goals that are yours, along with your belief in the ideas you have chosen. I believe that communicating background and data about yourself is as essential as marketing your business plans, because you and your venture are inseparable. You are the one who will be at the helm.

Transfer all pertinent information about yourself to point six of your plan. This restates what you earlier put on your Life/Work Chart, but presents it in a way to help market yourself and what you are doing, especially to potential backers, investors, or bankers.

A Summary of the Resources I Bring to My Enterprise

_____

_____

_____

_____

Your completed plan can be "lifted out" from this book and presented in a separate prospectus for your own reference, or for others who are interested. You have accomplished a *substantial* effort.

Writing out working plans has helped you consider all facets of your activity, and be aware of potential trouble spots early on. By preparing everything yourself, you should have more confidence and knowledge during the precarious phase of starting up. If you really believe you've identified a good idea, that opportunity need not pass you by because of lack of backing, financial or otherwise. Your ideas, properly organized, can assist in securing whatever support you need, and your plans, presented in prospectus form, can demonstrate a thoroughness that goes beyond the norm. Rarely will a banker, a friend, or an investment group see such a complete documentation for a proposed plan and activity. They can't help being impressed by your hard work and dedication.

Years ago when my husband and I started our own company we had youth, enthusiasm, and an idea for a venture we felt would be a good one. We were confronted, however, with not having the economic backing to start it in as professional a way as we would have liked.

We decided to present our idea to investors in the form of a business plan and prospectus, with the hope of raising any additional capital that was needed. We called on business leaders in the community who might be interested in investing in "a good idea" and discovered that obtaining money, while challenging, was not difficult. I feel that the integrity of our project, plus an organized approach to our efforts, enabled us to get the financial assistance that was necessary. This can be your experience too, because you are being thorough in your own planning.

It has been said that money flows to good ideas, and that if you have a money problem you really have an idea problem. Get the idea "right," and the backing will follow. Happily, I can report that over the years our plans did work out. My husband and I are grateful for the confidence that was placed in us, and for the many good people who helped us in our business as it grew through the years.

I don't know what kind of Life/Work you are thinking of, or what your ideas are, but don't let a need of outside help or money stop you. Search until you find a way and don't give up. The Small Business Administration can provide much assistance, at no cost to you. There are numerous pamphlets you can send for from any field office or from the Washington, D.C. headquarters, and they can also advise you financially. Many cities have local federal agencies and banks that have simplified their loan procedures and have a willingness to help you and help women in general. Smaller banks are especially taking advantage of these more difficult times in the 1990s, with many seeing an opportunity to help the small business entrepreneur.

Now that you have organized your ideas and put them down in a written plan, you are almost ready to start your venture/activity. Before you do, let's listen once more as another woman talks about her own start-up experiences. Joyce shares some of the personal challenges and actions she took as she began her enterprise, which was a service activity. In starting any new enterprise, emotional and work related issues seem to be inexorably intertwined. They are part of Joyce's life, and you may find them to be a part of your own experience.

Joyce's story is an interesting one. She started her activity in the down time of a job she already was holding. She was working at her local city hall first as a secretary and then as a child advocate, when she started to think about other things she could do. Joyce had been an advocate for nine years, a position she enjoyed and was proud of, especially considering she didn't have a college degree and had to prove herself to get the job. However, she was facing economic pressures and decided to look for something that could bring in extra income and use her abilities. Also, her two children were in a school system she didn't think was the best, and she wanted to be able to send them to a private school. This desire eventually led her to wonder whether she and her daughters could clean houses "on the side," and together save the money that the family needed for their personal needs and goals.

Joyce decided to put an ad in the paper and didn't realize at that time she was really starting a service business, nor did she realize that her one ad would lead to being fully involved in an activity of her own. Her children were not sure either whether they wanted their mother to clean houses, or whether they wanted to help her in that work. However, feeling she had no other workable solution, Joyce decided to go ahead with her plans. Here is how she started.

Joyce's Story

I put an ad in the paper offering housecleaning services, and I figured this was my children's future. It started out as a need to survive. I started cleaning houses, and one of the people I was cleaning for called the *Boston Globe* and suggested that they interview me. A woman from the *Globe* called and did interview me. They even wanted a picture. My children weren't sure about having a picture in the paper showing us cleaning! I decided fast I had better choose a name for my business, and thought of *Joy of*

Cleaning. My name in Italian is Gioa and in English, Joyce, which means Joy. This was exciting. The interview went well, and we were written up. I really didn't know what I was doing, though. My phone started ringing off the hook after the newspaper article. I was devastated by the phone calls, and had all kinds of calls for all kinds of things. But I kept a list, and wrote down the name, city, and phone number of each person. After that week of calls, I stopped answering the phone. I separated calls into cities, and since I couldn't go everywhere, I decided I would go where I could go easily.

I started having a full-fledged cleaning company. For my letterhead I cut out a picture of a house and building from the yellow pages, reproduced it, and printed my name on top. I visited clients with a clip board, introduced myself to them, listed their rooms and what I would do in each room, and gave them a price. At that point I still wasn't sure what to charge, but was glad to even get the work. I took on five houses a week to start off. Meanwhile I was still working at the office for children, and now doing cleaning either at night or early in the morning, and taking care of two teen-age daughters. There was a lot of pressure, but I realized that no one else was going to take care of me.

I began by cleaning myself and trying to find the quickest way to clean. I had to decide the most economical way to get the job done, for time and motion. I estimated what I could save in each room, and three to four minutes saved in each room, if there were six rooms, meant I was out of there half an hour sooner. If I couldn't do this, it would not be worth it.

My business has grown to where I have twelve girls working for me, and I have hired an accountant. The girls clean fifty homes a week, and ten commercial accounts. The business is still growing. My next goal is to get a van and to add a rug and upholstery cleaning service. I also would like to teach a course at a local college on, 'So You Want to Start a Cleaning Business.' All along I have tried to keep a log, with notes on how I solved problems.

Anyone who has a good idea should push it as far as they can. If they really have an idea they like, they should think through all the parts that could go wrong ahead of time. Think them out in their minds. If they picture something going wrong, they should ask themselves what would the solution be. And then solve it.

Joyce has reason to be proud of herself. Nothing was handed to her, and she had some difficult circumstances early in life. She married at nineteen and had to go on welfare for one month, an experience she remembers all too well. She said that was a humbling experience, and she dreaded going to pick up her check. She felt both an economic and an emotional stress. By pluck and by making her own luck, she pursued jobs she had no background in except that they used the abilities she had. Even the child advocate job was obtained in spite of the objections of someone who believed that the job should only go to someone who had a college education and not to "just a secretary." This in spite of the fact that Joyce was actually doing the job anyway. Joyce, through legally confronting the situation, was able to reverse the decision and have official approval for the advocate position. Later when she added her cleaning service to that occupation, she literally worked day and night to make her plans and goals come true. There was a lot of sacrificing for her and for her children. As I talked with Joyce I could sense her pride and all she had learned, and I think she will keep reaping the benefits of her own sacrifices and labors.

Your plans can direct you in your own start-up challenges. Next on your agenda is to answer and fill out questions relating to things yet to be accomplished. Such a list becomes a further extension of your business plan.

In the following chapter you will be asked questions that can relate to any start-up activity. You are closer to taking that important step of beginning the Life/Work you feel is ideal for you!

Chapter Six

Making Your Dreams a Reality

Whatever you do, work at it with all your heart, as working for the Lord, not for men.

Colossians 3:23

There are several factors to consider when you come to the actual start-up point of the venture creation process. Certain events or tasks usually signal the inception of a new venture. Many of these have been considered in all you have done so far, resulting in the writing of a business plan and now a master startup list.

Starting from scratch, or at a very modest level, is the easiest and lowest cost approach to doing anything, including starting a business. This is especially true if the activity you are planning lends itself to a small-scale, spare-time effort. Starting from where there was no foundation before also provides the freedom of choice to create what you wish and to shape it to your own liking, as you feel led to do. Your entire journey in this book has been about doing that very thing.

Start-up activities usually fall in one of two categories. The first is an activity or a business similar to others already in existence. Most opportunities fall in this category and yours most likely will, but with your personal stamp upon it. The second category concerns starting something that is unique in the service provided, in the product made, or in the way in which business is done. Both of these categories can benefit from a start-up list. Needless to say, a start-up similar to other ventures is easier to do, because there are precedents.

Begin then by looking at a master list of questions that can help in the formative stages of your activity. You can check off items that are relative to your activity, and note where you may need to gather more information. This list is a checklist against your own written plans! You may want to refer to those plans to get some of your answers. If you find it unnecessary to implement all the suggestions below, examining them in a step-by-step fashion will nevertheless help you think through whatever it is you are planning and doing. This list can also apply to nonbusiness, especially as it relates to any organizing that needs to be done.

Master Questions For a Start-up List

A. Questions about the Purpose of My Activity
  1. What is it I am selling or offering?
  2. Are others offering the same thing?
  3. Have I checked the Thomas Register, a listing of business by product or service, to see if my product or service is already being offered?
  4. How difficult would it be for someone to have the same idea?
  5. Can I discuss my idea with an expert in this area?
  6. Have I written an adequate statement of what I want to do for customers, employees, or suppliers to help them understand the purpose of my venture?

B. Questions about My Product
  1. If I am going to have a product, or merchandise, how much opening inventory is needed and at what cost?
  2. What product lines are available from suppliers? Are there alternative sources of supply? Are there volume discounts?

3. Do I need certain equipment or display fixtures?

4. How will I price my product? Are there markups for each type of item? Should there be an overall average markup?

5. Are there selling seasons to what I'm doing? How does this affect my plan?

6. Is there a second product or feature to my venture?

7. Do I know how to charge for each item I sell?

8. How is merchandise to be priced? Have I compared it to others?

9. Have I decided to price my product on the basis of the cost of it or on what competitors charge for it? Can I price it according to what the market will bear?

10. Is my pricing enough so I will make a profit?

11. Do I know what my contribution margin, or the ability of my product to generate revenue as its volume goes up or down, is; do I know where my break-even point is, or when I have profit?

12. Have I identified my market?

13. Do I know the methods of distribution?

C. Questions about My Service

1. Do I understand the nature of my service?

2. Do I understand the potential market with its needs and problems?

3. What will it take to sell my service?

4. If I'm doing a service for profit, will it make money?

5. Have I priced my service competitively?

6. Does this service have a unique feature to it, or a different way of filling a need?

7. Have I decided what location would best suit my service, based on competition, potential customers, and my own preference of home or otherwise?

8. Have I found the right niche to fill?

9. Do I know the unique services I plan to offer?

10. Have I discovered how to offer an intangible product and ways to promote it, through advertising or image?

11. Do I know the image I want to promote or feature?

D. Questions about Insurance, Legal, and Tax Matters
   1. Is there insurance that I should purchase and/or do I need liability insurance?
   2. Have I decided on a single legal form of organization, or researched all alternatives?
   3. Have I allowed for unpredictable expenses resulting from uninsured risks, like bad debts or fire?
   4. Have I complied with regulations regarding brand names, copyrighting, and trademarks?
   5. Have I gotten either a Social Security number or tax identification number for my venture?
   6. Have I complied with local town regulations by filing required forms with the town? Have I done the same for the State and Federal governments?
   7. Do I know a lawyer I can go to for advice with legal matters?

E. Questions about My Customers
   1. Have I defined my customer?
   2. Do I know how and why my "customer" uses or buys what I am offering?
   3. Are most of my customers local?
   4. Do I know where my customers "are"?
   5. Do I feel I can establish a permanent clientele and repeat customers?
   6. Do I know the message or media which will influence my customers?
   7. Do I know what kind of people will want what I am offering?
   8. Will I let my customers buy on credit?
   9. Can I obtain a commitment or sales order in advance from potential customers?

F. Questions about Market and Marketing
   1. Have I analyzed recent trends in this business?

2. Do I have a list of methods most suitable for reaching my market, and advertising my business?

3. Should I consider direct mail? Do I have a good mailing list?

4. Have I gone over marketing related issues with a marketing consultant or expert?

5. How will I advertise?

6. Do I understand what my major market is and what my minor market is?

7. What are the most important features and benefits of my "business" to promote?

8. What is the cost of the media or methods that I will use to advertise or promote my service?

9. What do others do to reach the same market I am trying to reach?

G. Questions about Competition

1. Who are my competitors or my nearest competitors?

2. Do they have a big share of the market, or are they a highly visible presence?

3. Do I have my competitor's advertising budget?

4. Should I anticipate having to raise or lower my price to meet competitors in the future?

H. Questions about Financing

1. How much money do I need for rent, equipment, salaries, inventory, and contingencies to start?

2. How much of my own money can be put into the venture, versus how much is needed?

3. How much credit can I get from my suppliers, the people I will buy from?

4. Can I borrow the rest of the money needed to start my venture, and what are the going interest rates and repayment terms?

5. Can I raise money by getting venture capital?

6. Can I figure out what net income per year I expect to get from my activity if that is a goal?

7. Have I talked to a banker about my plans?

8. Do I need to talk to an accountant about my plans?

9. Do I have financial statements ready?

10. Have I planned a system of records that will keep track of my income and expenses—what I will owe others and what they will owe me?

11. Have I found a way to keep payroll records and to take care of tax reports and payments?

12. Do I know what my largest expense items are, and can they be controlled?

13. Do I have a budget that can handle the unexpected?

14. How much does incorporation cost? If I incorporate, should it be regular or sub-chapter S for tax purposes? (Where income or losses can be recognized on my personal tax return.)

This is a long list, but these questions can be important depending on what your own start-up requirements are. If what you are doing is unlike anything else, many of the questions above will be the same; but if there were no customers, competitors, or suppliers to talk to, you would be facing a greater challenge. This would suggest doing some test marketing with a small sample of your product being sold through limited outlets, often on a consignment basis. Or, if you have a service, you could do test marketing with a questionnaire to prospective customers, interviewing them to get their honest reaction and responses to your service plans. This can show whether your service is needed or is of value, or whether it could be improved upon.

If there are proprietary natures to your service or product, when something new is being done, there are legal procedures that can protect your ideas. Products can be patented, and brand names, trademarks and copyrights are available. It is not commonly known, but there is an even better way to protect your idea. The U.S. Patent Office has a "Disclosure Document" registration program. This allows you to write up an idea that may or may not lead to a patent, and protect it through a registration process for a two-year period.

Finding Answers to Your Questions

Where do you get answers to the questions on your start-up list? If they aren't in your written plans, you will have to talk to outside sources that can help you. Three sources that can be especially good are: major customers, major suppliers, and even major competitors or small business owners and entrepreneurs. There are also secondary sources of information, such as trade associations, the Better Business Bureau, the Chamber of Commerce, the Small Business Association, distributors, manufacturer's representatives, competitor's customers or any person or organization that comes in contact with the activity you are beginning.

Talking to the right people can be an enormous benefit. As my husband was starting our business, one person he talked with gave him an idea on how to sell his label product through distributors, instead of through a direct sales force. That *one* idea helped him build a business that eventually carved out a unique market and distribution system in the industry. All from one person and one idea. Don't underestimate the help others can give you, or that one good idea can bring to your efforts. Identifying the right people and asking the right questions is an importrant part of your marketing analysis. Most people like to be helpful and are even flattered when you seek them out.

We have spent a lot of time describing business strategies and their practical application to help you manage your life and life's work. It is exciting to realize too that God has plans for you, and has His own ideas for your well being and happiness. "For I know the plans I have for you . . . plans to prosper you and not to harm you, plans to give you hope and a future" (Jeremiah 29:11). If your journey to discover a meaningful Life/Work has been one marked by reliance on God from the very beginning, that activity should represent God's plans and hopes for your own future.

With the conclusion of your Master Start-up List, you can turn your attention to writing out a Start-up Schedule. (This is a refining of your list and a putting into action of much that was on it.) We will follow the guidelines of a schedule for a business, but again, your activity will determine what you put on your schedule and even the order you put it in. The implementation of a schedule will itself be a factor in moving your venture forward.

Before you write a schedule, let's hear Franca discuss what she did as she got her enterprise off and going, and what that event meant to her. Franca is originally from Milan, but she and her husband have been in this country for many years. She describes her feelings about managing her creative venture in the United States.

Franca's Story

I had an academic background until I began my venture in the States. In Europe I was taking care of family, children, and entertaining. Now in the U.S. for some time, I hoped to do something else. An idea came to me about five years ago. I was helping friends in Italy who wanted to see if their clothing products were marketable in the States. I took some of their samples and called on retail stores until I got an order. I had custom coats and gave shops the ability to have their own line made up for them, and to be exclusive in what they were offering. I would go to Italy two times a year to select the items and to personalize high fashion. The idea went well.

Then I decided I wanted to have everything from coats to a total wardrobe, and to personalize that too and make it exclusive. My belief was that all women should be able to look good. In the regular store clients can select the style and size for them, but in a private showing they can select the style, the exact color, and a fit that was tailored just for them. A custom fitting woman would make the difference. I decided to make this service available. I would send orders to Milan to be made, and in four weeks they would come back to the U.S. and another fitting would be done. Each dress would be personalized for the individual client's taste and proportions.

Location was important. In Europe if a woman wanted a custom dress she would go to a shop called *L'atelier*. It was always in a private location, in a court or in a nice downtown building. The place would be elegant, and an appointment was necessary. I, therefore, wanted to offer a similar experience and have a good setting and a by-invitation-only fashion showing, with models wearing the clothing I was trying to sell. My prices would not be astronomical, because I would not have the overhead of a store. I would ask women for fifty percent down payment to cover expenses, and later collect the rest upon receiving the items ordered.

I know most of my clients so when I order my samples for my fall or spring show, I can select dresses with certain clients in mind. I think what I am doing is fascinating. I see new styles, new names every day in fashion. Fashion is dictated from Europe, and especially Milan now, whereas it used to be Paris. I also think it is important to know both worlds, the U.S. and Europe.

Being in the States and dealing with American women gives me the desire to go ahead, because America is a country that is woman-oriented. I feel good to be here. It is a wonderful feeling for a woman to start an activity. Any woman can start. Over here you are accepted and get positive results. In Europe for a woman it is hard to begin, and if she does she often finds that people are pleasant, but she never gets anywhere with what she is doing. You have to be introduced by someone and go through a long corridor of "steps" before you are received. This usually means special training or education in addition. Here you can make a phone call, introduce yourself, explain what your service is, and have someone say, "Come by soon and show me." I did this, and in one meeting with a store, was able to place thousands of dollars worth of orders. It made me feel good, and it is so different from Europe.

I am not selling just because I want to sell. What I get from what I'm involved in is more than I get from anything else. I am accepted with no background in business, and I have a very harnessed approach. Basically before this I had never worked in my life. I think, however, that when you have a good product, even with no experience, and believe in yourself, you can find a way to express yourself in an activity.

A Typical Start-up Schedule
Let's look at some of the steps for starting your own enterprise. Combining this "business" schedule with Franca's approach to thinking and planning should be helpful to you. This is a condensation of your start-up list, focusing on the most urgent or important items to be done.
1. Refining of the business plan for securing start-up financing.
2. Incorporation into whatever legal organization you have decided on.
3. Obtaining a business license (when needed).
4. Developing a record keeping system.
5. Determining a pricing schedule (as needed).
6. Deciding on a name and on an advertising strategy.
7. Making needed purchases of supplies or inventory/ equipment.
8. Choosing a location or determining site location.
9. Doing any market analysis still necessary to identify

key suppliers and sources of distribution, etc.

10. Determining the people needs, inside or out.

As we go over this schedule, you can refer to both your business plan and "check-off" start-up list, and address the steps that apply to your activity. This is basically information you've recorded, but you are reorganizing the key elements for start-up. If you aren't planning on starting a business or a profit enterprise, you can still benefit from refining your financial requirements, from deciding on a name (for a nonprofit activity), from keeping records, from doing a marketing analysis, and so on. Such a schedule can help coordinate any endeavor or work.

My Start-up Schedule

1. Refine the business plan in order to obtain initial financing. If arranging financing is necessary, you can tailor your business plan and do a second plan that can be used to show bankers or investors. This is a compact version of the overall plan you have written, but presents it for use as a financial tool. Points to be included if you decide to refine and write out a shorter plan for the purposes of seeking economic assistance are:

a. A statement of the purpose of your activity, and all pertinent literature and brochures (this you have addressed).

b. A description of the structure of your activity and the "product" or "service" envisioned (this also you have completed).

c. A statement of how money is going to be used, how much is being sought, and how it can be repaid (if not a business, show what monies are required and why).

d. A resumé of your background and experience, and business financial statement (already done).

e. A statement of the projected income and expenses for the next two years (if this applies).

f. A description of your competition, with an evaluation

of your plans and outlook for the future (there can be competition in a non-business activity).

g. A demonstration that you have sufficient insurance (if this applies).

h. A sales forecast in dollars (if this applies).

Bear in mind as you look for financial aid that two types of financing are available to you, debt and equity, and therefore two methods of raising start-up capital or seed money. If you decide on debt financing or on a loan, you will have to explain your intentions of repaying that money and show what collateral you have. You do, however, maintain control over your enterprise. If you decide on equity financing, be prepared to show an investor whether stock purchased will increase in value and why. You don't have a legal obligation to pay back investment money, but by giving up equity in your venture you are also giving part of it away.

You'll have to think about what is best for you. Either way you should proceed with an attitude of confidence in your plans and in yourself. If you're going to a bank, shop them as carefully as they will you. The choice of a bank may be one of your most important decisions. With all the work you've done, you don't have to go "hat in hand." If banks should turn you down, you can always go to the Small Business Administration and if you can prove that you couldn't raise funds in any other way, they may give you a loan.

2. Decide on a legal organization. Have you determined whether your activity requires a legal organization? Are you going to have a sole proprietorship, where you alone own and manage your activity? There is little legal requirement for this, but you are personally liable for all claims, which could mean your personal property. You have to pay a self-employment tax. Another type of organization is a partnership, both general and limited. The general partnership is a sole proprietorship, and needs no registration.

The limited permits investors to become partners, and they only risk as much as they invest. The limited partnership must have at least one general partner, who does have unlimited liability.

The third form of legal organization is the corporation. You as a stockholder are removed from any personal liability. You do have your stock to lose. Incorporation, however, can be costly, extensive record keeping is necessary, and corporate taxation is heavy. You will need a lawyer's help with incorporating. There is a sub-chapter S corporation (with up to ten stockholders) which can be attractive to anyone in a smaller venture.

3. Obtain a business license. Depending on your situation, license requirements vary according to each city and state. You can call your city hall or state licensing bureau to ascertain this.

4. Set up business books or develop a record-keeping system. This is needed if you are starting any type of business, and some record-keeping can be good for volunteer or nonbusiness activities. Books or records need to be established that tell you how much you owe people and how much they owe you, and also tell you how much money you have invested in equipment or merchandise. You can list what your expenses are and show your gross margin.

Bookkeeping doesn't apply just to financial records. You will need nonfinancial records, such as inventory and purchasing records. How do you set up your bookkeeping? There are many record keeping systems already available, prepackaged in stationery stores. The SBA has a pamphlet, MA.1.017, "Keeping Records in a Small Business." Or you can retain the services of a bookkeeping service, or accountant.

5. Determine a pricing schedule. If you have a product to be priced you should determine the exact cost of labor

and materials for each item. You would multiply that figure by the number of items you hope to sell in a year. Then you would add this to your entire overhead for the year. You may have figured your pricing as you went over your start-up list of essentials. Bear in mind your pricing policy should not be so low as to not cover expenses, nor so high as to not be competitive, or be able to build volume.

There may be typical gross margin figures for certain products. Competitive and marketing strategies may mean you have different gross margins for the type of product or service you are offering. Competitive products may have only a ten percent margin, where other items may have gross margins as high as forty to fifty percent. Margins are there to make a profit, and also to provide for the unanticipated or for hidden costs.

You don't always have to climb down the price ladder either, if you understand what is unique about your activity, and if you can promote that uniqueness, no matter what it is. (Many people often don't understand and capitalize on that uniqueness.) Pricing should always represent value to a "customer," as well as cost to the supplier.

6. Decide on a name and an advertising strategy. If you are choosing a name, the name you pick should give others an indication of the area you are concentrating in and what you are doing. A name can be used for any enterprise, be it a product, service, or volunteer activity. That name is strongly tied to whatever image or benefits you want to project. It should conjure up the feelings, moods, impulses you want to elicit from others. Don't make it coy or gimmicky. I once saw a gift shop called "Present Perfect" and thought that was a good name, because it clearly stated what the shop was about. Another name that caught my attention, this time for a volunteer activity, was "Helping Hand." This group's name expressed its goal of helping the elderly and others through volunteer assistance.

What will your advertising strategy be if you need one?

Will you be using newspaper, magazine, or radio ads? Advertising can help establish your name, create an image, and make your venture visible. Budget projections for the year should include two to five percent of your annual gross volume for advertising. Service activities may require more. Advertising should be consistent and should reinforce the overall purpose of your activity. Finally, it should tell people how you can meet their needs. If you have a nonbusiness venture, ask yourself if advertising applies and, if so, how you could advertise.

7. Make purchases or order supplies and inventory. Did you decide from your start-up list if you needed to order supplies? This can be anything from stationery and order forms to equipment or inventory of needed products or materials. Figure out how much you need, when it should be ordered, and if there are any discounts available. Supplies may also be needed for a nonbusiness activity.

8. Determine site location and space needs. If your activity is to be in your home, you can save on rent, utilities, and furnishings. Expenses for a home "office" can be deducted from your income tax, if that office is not used for other purposes, such as a TV room.

If you are going to work outside your home, you should choose a location that is suitable for what you are doing. Four factors can determine a successful site location: *the amount of traffic, income, competition in the area,* and the *convenience and visibility of the site.* These cannot be stressed enough. However, you don't want to take on too much overhead and give your profits to a landlord.

You should be able to justify your choice of location in your working plans and in your financial projections. Allocate about six percent of your intended sales volume for rent.

The SBA and the Chamber of Commerce can help you with some of these decisions.

9. Do any necessary additional market analysis. If marketing is valuable in the beginning stages to bring your ideas to market or to fruition, be sure you know such things as:
- key suppliers
- sources of distribution
- key site-selection factors
- existing competitive services or products
- start-up costs

These items may call for doing more market analysis and research. Have get-acquainted meetings with your key suppliers, or visit with key and potential customers. You may also contact the team of people we mentioned—bankers, accountants, lawyers, trade associations and the SBA.

10. Determine the people both inside and outside you need to help start up, regardless of what kind of enterprise you have.

Will you need others? Decide ahead of time the tasks to be done, the needed skills, the knowledge called for, and determine the people who will cover each area of responsibility. Together, they will make a team essential to your success. Some of these people can be drawn from the outside, as consultants or freelancers, rather than requiring space under your roof and a weekly paycheck, since their contributions may only be called for at certain times. We found this to work very well in our own business. Outside people can bring a fresh perspective. We really appreciated the help received from them and benefited from their expertise. You can also outline the services of people who can contribute in other ways. They could be suppliers, networking contacts, friends, or other businesses.

When a start-up schedule has been completed, you can consider starting your enterprise. The challenge at that point will be twofold: getting your venture off to a good start, or getting business in the door, or both.

You'll need to write a charter for your newly structured

venture-activity that can provide a sense of direction, just as you earlier filled out a Life/Work Chart giving direction to your life. This charter will define your project's goals and define its future as well. Such definition will help you to always be able to ask, "Am I making progress according to my plans?" Your charter should state a clear purpose and an overview of your activity, along with what you want to accomplish. The definition of your venture and its purpose will form the charter for your enterprise.

My Life/Work Charter

_____

_____

_____

_____

_____

To show the benefits of having a charter, let's look at a practical application. If your purpose originally was to create something of beauty for others to enjoy, and the purpose of your chosen venture was to create high quality craft items for the home, your personal and professional purposes obviously would be in concert.

Your charter would also tell you not to be tempted to add craft items later that weren't up to the same standards (resisting the temptation to mass produce and lower the quality of what is being offered), and not to allow your product to be sold in places where other gift products would fail to reflect the same craftsmanship and excellence. The path or course of action for you and your enterprise in the future would be steered by the rudder of your intended mission. What you do will continue to be an outgrowth of your original purposes. Even more, you will be assured of an ongoing belief in your efforts and work.

Adhering to a written purpose or charter for an activity

until that purpose can be enlarged, as time and opportunity permit, seems like common sense. However, you may find that you've no sooner declared your goals, than those goals are put to the test. I recall when I was first involved in Mill Falls Studio deciding we would make a high-end ornament line, with an emphasis on custom-designed art. Within a very short time we were being pressured by those in our distribution system to also place our product in low-end retail stores. This would have given our gift line much more exposure, but would have been incompatible with the goals and image we wanted to maintain. It is important to know what you are trying to do and stick to your guns, because there will be many temptations not to.

If your venture is volunteer or nonprofit oriented, a charter can be equally important. If your charter expresses a purpose/mission of caring for the elderly, you would not be tempted later to extend your activity to other endeavors, well meaning though they may be. In a volunteer effort there may not be economic reasons to "sell out" or abandon your mission ideas, but there can easily be emotional reasons to do so. If you are giving of yourself, others may

**Writing
a Mission Charter**

impose upon that "gift," and assume you can give to many different causes or people. You have to decide what means the most to you, and where you want to use your talents and energies. A charter will insure you stay on course.

Beginning Your Venture

The challenge as you begin will be to express your mission, or reason for being, throughout your enterprise and in any related outside functions. Here too you may be defining new concepts or ways of doing things, redefining work. Traditionally the purpose of a business has been to create a "customer," but your purpose may set forth a different standard. You can have an activity in which your goal is to create customers, but this does not have to be your main purpose. Your venture has been designed to comply with your own desires, as you stretched the concept of what that venture could be. You may be doing it for reasons of equal importance to you—personal growth and satisfaction, helping others, or a philanthropic public-spirited contribution.

Are there any remaining factors that could contribute to the success of your efforts? While one of the most crucial variables affecting success is the actual choice of the service or product being offered, there are other things that can contribute to success. Being in the "right business or right place at the right time" is one. Still others are more personal factors of strong motivation, of building on experiences and achievements, of having goals, and of recognizing an opportunity. All these you have been careful to include, in addition to trusting God for your life's work and the fulfilling of your dreams and plans.

Yes, there are business factors that can also enhance chances for success. They are:
- continuing to see the wants and needs of people
- knowing a business and a market thoroughly
- having adequate capital
- keeping good records

—having profitable pricing

—delivering value to customers and keeping them happy

—maintaining integrity in everything

But those points too have been covered in your planning. There isn't a stone you've left unturned.

Further ways you could cut down on risk and increase your chances for a successful activity, as we mentioned earlier, would be to start your activity on a part-time basis, while still tending to your home or still keeping a job. It can be done in the after hours of a job as Joyce did when beginning her housecleaning service and while holding her advocacy job. Or your activity can be done in the after hours as wife and mother, as some of the women in this book have done. This approach lends itself to a variety of Life/Work choices. As suggested before, you could start on a small scale in one specific area. Bigger does not always mean better. You can minimize your risk too by keeping your overhead down, meaning fixed costs like rent, employees, decorating and equipment. Too much overhead is a constant danger to any enterprise.

Finally, you could do a best case/worst case scenario, by asking yourself once more, "What have I got to lose?" and "What have I got to gain?" In business, downside risk refers to how much the business stands to lose if it fails, and upside to how much it stands to gain if it succeeds. It is the same for your own upside and downside potentials, and for that of your enterprise or venture.

Webster defines an enterprise as "an undertaking, especially a big, bold, or difficult one." Venture is defined as, "a risky undertaking, as in business, something on which a risk is taken."[1] These definitions describe more the possible outcome rather than the actual endeavor, and the outcome is colored heavily with negative overtones. This doesn't have to be the case for you, but that isn't to say you won't have struggles or challenges, both personal and otherwise. It would be wrong to suggest differently. There is work involved and a certain amount of risk. However, if you are working with all your heart for God (and not for people), that makes a big difference. Everything you do becomes worthwhile.

Nothing is more exciting than to move out and to begin to capture your dreams. When you finally get a chance to build a new or better way of life, or to discover a new vocation, your desire to do that coupled with your faith in God can more than see you through. The payoffs can be great: finding new ways to use your talents, discovering a creative activity or project that you could truly enjoy — while reaping the kind of personal reward that can bring, — and finally, helping others as you fulfill your own purposes and goals for your life. Few things can be as satisfying as doing something which is the very essence of yourself. And last, but certainly not least, discovering God's plan for your life and future.

Chapter Seven

Putting Yourself on the Line

I am the Lord your God, who teaches you what is best
for you, who directs you in the way you should go.

Isaiah 48:17

You are about to launch the creative enterprise of your
choice. In doing that you have another journey ahead of
you just in providing a service or in offering a product that
can successfully meet the needs of others. That journey
will also take you into yet-to-be-explored territory, both
personally and professionally.

In directing a Life/Work centered around your own talents and developing your core of self, you are becoming
one of the women not only redefining women's tasks and
work, but redefining women's role and "woman" herself.
Women like yourself are expressing the innate qualities
and capacities that women have, qualities that are more
and more coming into full bloom. Especially exciting is to
see that blossoming occurring under the guidance of God-
directed tasks. Many women, and indeed creative people
throughout history, have long attributed "God in their
work" as that which lifts their work to a higher level, and
brings an excellence beyond their own. Catherine Marshall
said it well:

When achievement has come because of our helplessness linked to God's power, it has a rightness about it

that no amount of self-inspired striving can
have . . . because we know that ideas and the ability to
implement them flowed into us from somewhere beyond our selves, we can be objective about our good
fortune. . . . God has never allowed me the fulfillment
of a soul's sincere desire without first putting me
through an acute realization of my inadequacy and my
need for help.[1]

I certainly would second Catherine Marshall's thoughts. I
believe helplessness doesn't preclude a sense of adventure
and pioneering, but having an adventuresome spirit also
doesn't preclude a dependency on God. I would be the first
to say that without that dependence I would not have been
able to accomplish my own goals.

For each of us there is only one thing necessary: to fulfill
our own destiny, according to God's will, and to be what
God wants us to be. Our gifts, especially our unused gifts,
cry out to be used and recognized, and to be given a name.
Our fullest potentials continue to be brought into existence
only as we exercise the abilities that we have. This process
also provides the experience of growing toward wholeness.
Much of the work of growing up is finding our center and
integrating our creative parts.

As you take the final step of starting the activity that
draws on your own talents and motivations, let's hear
again from women who have integrated their work, faith,
and abilities in a satisfying Life/Work. You can see how
they felt about risking and stretching themselves as they
faced the same challenges you are confronted with.

Andrea's Story

I design flower arrangements, which came from my
interest in designing. I always had the creative sense
of wanting to design something, and have designed a
lot of other things in my lifetime. I fell into working
with flowers as part of another job I had as a buyer in

a store that had a flower shop. I realized flower arranging was the best use of all my talents. Once I started it felt like the best thing I had ever done. I felt really at home with it.

I tried to approach my work more professionally, and decided to take a course. Upon completion I got another job working with silk flowers. My boss, a woman, saw I had good ideas and encouraged me. My abilities grew as I was able to express myself in my own way with freedom. I developed outside things, and wanted to branch out.

I started my own wedding business using silk and fresh flowers, and also worked with another woman who rents wedding clothing and wanted someone to enhance her shop with flower arrangements. Now I have an ongoing activity with my own clients. Out of this has come a wholesale enterprise with decorative products for the home, capitalizing on the Victorian influence—wreaths, English oval wreaths, posy hangings on the wall and so on. My customers are stores throughout New York and private individuals, in addition to decorators who need my services. I make a lot of silk flowers which to me is the ultimate art form.

I think this is the first time in my life that I have done something with a God-given gift. It has made me happier than anything I've ever done in my life. There is a security in working with God-endowed talents because it means you are inherently good at it. Your self image isn't threatened. The decorative arts industry is highly competitive, and a person could probably not do well unless she were sure of herself.

Once you get in touch with "something" you innately are good at, each step builds on the previous step, not as part of your own control, but more as the natural sequence of a talent growing and an activity unfolding. The world wants more. You get better and better.

I feel strongly about having people find what they

are given as natural talents. You should look for what you do well, and admit you do well at it. God gave me the right to say that, because He gave me my abilities. This is good to know, because then things don't depend on me—there is already a foundation. It helps me to take risks. I want to try for the next higher step in what I am doing.

Having my own creative activity is so exciting—it is like giving birth again.

Andrea obviously believes that it has been more than worth any challenges met or labor expended to use her own creativity and find that which could really motivate her. Of interest is that she doesn't look upon that process as a personal struggle, but as an outgrowth of the development of her talents and God's plans for those talents. That too seems to be a "natural" occurrence in her life. Andrea demonstrates a quiet and strong faith. She inspired me, and perhaps she will inspire you as you start your enterprise.

Andrea reminded me too of Leslie and her enthusiasm for "Send a Friend." I thought it would be appropriate to ask Leslie what she felt she has gained from her own undertaking. Does it continue to be worth her time and talents, and is it meeting her needs?

Leslie's Story

I have just returned from a visit with an individual who was slightly depressed the last time we met together. While contemplating today's visit and praying for a new creative idea to implement, I happened to remember a particular uplifting phrase, "When life hands you lemons, make LEMONADE!" So, my young children and I made a computerized, bright yellow six-foot-long banner, with bright sun designs and a saying printed across the front. Then we filled the beautiful pitcher with lemonade, sliced lemons, and ice.

When I hung the banner in her room, presented the lemonade and encouraged that person this morning with those words, I could immediately tell that the lemonade approach was indeed perfect for the moment. The expression on her face, and actually the entire visit came alive because of the 'lemonade' personal touch.

This business is a way of life for me. Every day the joys of serving other people far outweigh the pressures of the nitty-gritty intricacies of running a venture, because I am fulfilling the inner part of me that cries out to share with others. There have been moments when I have felt guilty and have even condemned myself for being ME. The fact that I have always been overly friendly, and tended to treat other people as if they were my long-lost buddies, has helped me realize that I am made this way. Neglecting my basic need of friendly expression only hurts ME.

I would encourage any woman who wishes to find a creative outlet for herself to analyze just what "makes her tick," and to write down talents, characteristics, and virtues which people have regularly complimented her on throughout her life—then develop a simple plan as to how that talent or virtue can best serve people.

I am determined that my enterprise will be a service of high quality, with the public learning very quickly that I can be trusted to "go the extra mile" in caring for others. Any challenges I have had, or you will have, will more than be outweighed by being able to offer honest and caring service. That is fundamentally what we all are looking for, and will stand the test of time.

Let's also listen to Pat's story. Pat is thirty-two years old, single, and has had only herself and her faith to rely on as she slowly developed what she most wanted to do.

Pat's Story

I have been doing a variety of activities. Basically I'm a free-lance makeup artist and stylist and I work with a variety of photographers, video and film production companies, and with a cable TV show. To supplement my income sometimes when I'm not doing makeup, I contract work out to a company that makes video games, and do data entry on a computer. I've done many different things to be self-supporting and I don't have parents to depend on. My father is not living and my mother is not able to provide economic help. This has enabled me, however, to be responsible for myself. I need to make sure, however, I have a consistent flow of income, which can be difficult when I am working as a free-lance artist.

I like my work. I feel I'm making people look better and feel better about themselves. My makeup business is a first priority, careerwise. I can fit it into any lifestyle I grow into. I also enjoy the freedom and being able to use my artistic and creative talent. I can work as little or as much as I want to. This activity suits me.

I've paid my dues. It's been a slow process to be where I'm at, but I've chosen that way because it was more comfortable to go slowly. I initially started doing makeup on the side, when I had a full time job in the stock market. For six years I worked in the market. During that time I would take personal and vacation days off to do my makeup business.

While in my stock market job my business gradually built up a clientele to where I needed more freedom than a full-time job could give me. I left to work a short time for a temporary agency, doing office work, so that I could put the makeup business as a higher priority. It gradually became fifty percent of my income.

I am now closer to doing makeup free-lancing as a

full-time venture. Being a free-lance artist often can be feast or famine. It's a good feeling to know when famine hits I can still support myself.

I want to open myself up to a lot of opportunities and I can see this business possibly leading into a career in film or television production. I'm also hoping for a family and children to be the main focus of my life. I feel God has a plan for me and I'm here to follow out that plan. I don't know what the plan is, He does, and He wants me to be happy.

I admire Pat's commitment to finding the way to slowly and carefully build the creative activity that she most wanted to do. Some have called her "lucky," and others wondered long ago why she didn't get a regular job and have more security. Pat chose instead to not give up her dream, and to do whatever she could do to insure that dream would come true. And she has still further plans for the future.

Leslie, Andrea, Pat, and others whose stories we've heard, as well as the untold numbers of women who every day dream new dreams, who are daring, risking, and assuming responsibility for their lives, join you as you begin to follow your own dreams and do things that you may never have dreamed of before.

A Shared Journey and Spirit

Wouldn't it be nice if we could hear from every woman who is taking a journey to discover her God-given resources and to find ways to put them to greater use? Time and space would not permit it, nor could we uncover them all. One story would be of Marian, a Native American from New Mexico. Marian recently started her own pottery making and tour-guide venture, using her interest in her heritage to both offer Southwestern crafts and to help educate others. She makes various pottery objects indigenous to the area she lives in, and she takes people sightseeing to places representing the Indian culture, such as a Kiva (worship place) or cave dwellings. Marian is a soft-spoken person with a deep, abiding trust in God and a keen understanding of people, history, and nature. She captivated me and the friends who were in my tour group, as she told of her plans. She showed me how women are one in spirit and aspirations, regardless of their backgrounds or individual abilities.

Again and again we read of women who voice thoughts and desires so much like our own. I have found, whether at home or traveling, I often pick up the newspaper or hear on television of yet another woman expressing the quest and journey so many of us are on. I read in the *Boston Globe* about Eileen Goudge, who told of her own challenges. She started her interview by saying, "I'm telling you all about my life because I don't want people to think failure is final." Eileen did not have the easiest of lives, having once been an abused wife, on welfare, and divorced twice. She now is married to famous literary agent Al Zuckerman. Eileen states:

> The valleys I went through strengthened me for any future adversity. No matter what happens, I know I can survive. . . . I was poor, but I had something no one could take away from me: imagination. I used it. I created scenarios. It's called daydreaming. Wanting something so much can actually make it happen. Your desire creates its own momentum. I believe in destiny. What it takes is being inner-directed. You have to define exactly what you want to achieve and move steadily toward the goal. When you get down to it, the bottom line is this: daydreams don't have to turn to dust.

This is the same Eileen Goudge whose first hardback novel, *Garden of Lies*, was the subject of a bidding war and sold to a publisher for $1 million. ABC-TV bought the rights for a miniseries. This in spite of the fact that an editor of a major publishing firm once told her she didn't have talent. Eileen concluded, "But I proved she was wrong."[2]

In 1990, the television program *Twenty/Twenty* featured a story on women divorcing after sixty, and the special circumstances they encountered. These women were suddenly alone in the world, sometimes floundering. Barbara Walters concluded the program by saying, "You've got to have something that's your own to fall back on."

Marian, Eileen, the many women in this book, and the women we will never meet as we each pursue something of our own, form an ever-increasing throng of women stretching, growing, accomplishing as they turn the pages of life. They are undaunted in their efforts, perhaps even unsung heroes, although I'm sure they don't think of themselves that way.

Following Dreams

Pursuing one's dreams, using one's talents, trusting God, seeking excellence in all one does, offering caring service, may require a period of personal testing previously unexperienced. Neglecting this pursuit may mean a more leisurely or pain-free existence, or even the pleasures of a daily life marked mostly by comfort and ease. But I believe that gaining one's heart's desire and growing as a person more than compensate for any difficulties encountered along the way. Even to have tried to achieve is an accomplishment and growth experience.

The journey you are taking also may include a testing by God to see whether you will depend on Him. That dependence we spoke of is a continuing part of your ongoing journey. You may have to let go of certain dreams, and allow them to follow a natural course. "Letting go" may actually precede their fulfillment. Often one does not hold on to one's dreams loosely. If anything, those dreams can be consuming. I had to remind myself that God was in charge of my dreams and my life, and rest in that understanding. It is a lesson that one does not always easily learn. Your dreams may not always work out just as you planned, or be on your timetable. You will know, however, you have done your best. It has been said that the true test of our dreams' maturity lies in our ability to give those dreams back to God. They may change, and we may not always take the path we had planned, but our dreams will be in good hands. God promises again in Isaiah to show what is best for us and to direct us "in the way we should go." We sometimes forget that exciting promise.

As you start on another journey in beginning your own creative activity or enterprise, you will need to keep your dreams and goals ever before you. Dreams and hopes can fade quickly, and never more so than when times of testing come. May you persevere in those times. Putting yourself on the line, and your dreams and your faith to the test, is to give a new visibility to all and, as always, to risk. It is also to be vulnerable.

Eventually, with the fulfillment of your goals and Life/ Work choices, the struggle and pain, much like the birth process itself, will fade with the joy of a new creation. This could be when your excitement and wonder really begin, as you see not just how far your talents, but even more, God's plans for those talents, will take you. Won't it be exciting to find out?

Remember, as you continue on your journey and follow that quest, you are not alone. Happy journeying . . . and God's best!

MY LIFE/WORK CHART

I. Who am I?

   A. My purpose/mission/motivation

_____

_____

_____

_____

_____

   B. My resources/abilities

_____

_____

_____

_____

   C. My uniqueness

_____

_____

_____

_____

II. Where Do I Want To Go?

A. My creative dream of what I'd like to do with my life.

_____

_____

_____

_____

_____

B. My focused dream goal of what I want to become or do.

_____

_____

_____

_____

_____

III. How Can I Get There?

A. My best strategy for getting where I want to go.

_____

_____

_____

_____

_____

B. My risk/reward ratio

   1. What I feel I have to offer or can risk.

_____

_____

_____

_____

_____

   2. What I feel I have to gain.

_____

_____

_____

_____

_____

C. A description of the type of activity I feel could present an acceptable risk factor.

_____

_____

_____

_____

_____

IV. My Creative Activity or Life/Work

A. The definition of my ideal activity.

_____

_____

_____

_____

_____

B. The goal of my venture.

_____

_____

_____

_____

V. The Charter For My Life/Work Activity

Restate the purpose or mission of my venture. This purpose should be compatible with my declared mission and goals. It is my charter, or road map, for the future.

_____

_____

_____

_____

_____

Notes

Chapter 1
1. *Mademoiselle.*
2. Baruch, Barnett, and Rivers, *Lifeprints* (McGraw-Hill, New York, N.Y., 1983).
3. *Time* Magazine (Special Issue, "Women: The Road Ahead," Fall, 1990).
4. Betty Freidan, *The Feminine Mystique* (New York: W.W. Norton & Company, Inc., 1963).
5. Colette Dowling, *The Cinderella Complex* (New York: Summit Books, 1981).
6. *Time* Magazine (Special Issue, "Women: The Road Ahead, Fall, 1990).
7. *Webster's New World Dictionary* (New York: Warner Books, 1983).
8. Anne Morrow Lindbergh, *Gift From the Sea* (New York: Pantheon Books, 1955).

Chapter 2
1. Ralph Mattson and Arthur Miller, *Finding a Job You Can Love* (New York: Thomas Nelson Publishers, 1982).
2. Helen Keller, *Hellen Keller Journal*, 1938.
3. Richard Nelson Bolles, *What Color Is Your Parachute?* (Berkeley, California: Ten Speed Press, 1990).
4. Abraham H. Maslow, *Toward a Psychology of Being* (New York: D. Van Nostrand Company, 1968).

Chapter 3
1. " 'Have I Done Well?' Understanding God's Will in Midlife," *Christianity Today* (February 17, 1989, p. 22).
2. Hannah Whitall Smith, *The Christian's Secret of a Happy Life* (New Jersey: Fleming H. Revell Co., 1870) p. 70.
3. Catherine Marshall, *Beyond Our Selves* (New York: McGraw-Hill Book Company, Inc., 1961) p. 176.

Chapter 4
1. Richard Bolles, *What Color Is Your Parachute?* (Berkeley, California: Ten Speed Press, 1990).
2. Ralph Mattson and Arthur Miller, *Finding A Job You Can Love* (New York: Thomas Nelson Publishers, 1982).
3. Elizabeth O'Connor, *Eighth Day of Creation* (Waco, Texas: Word Books, 1971).
4. Theodore Leavitt, *Innovation in Marketing* (New York: McGraw-Hill Book Company, 1962).
5. *Webster's New World Dictionary* (New York: Warner Books, 1983).

Chapter 6
1. *Webster's New World Dictionary* (New York: Warner Books, 1983).

Chapter 7
1. Catherine Marshall, *Beyond Our Selves*, (New York: McGraw-Hill Book Company, Inc., 1961) p. 158.
2. Eileen Goudge, *Boston Globe* (May 1989).